Hannes Wiher

**Holistic Mission**

# World of Theology Series

# Published by the Theological Commission of the World Evangelical Alliance

## Volume 25

Vol 1   Thomas K. Johnson: The First Step in Missions Training: How our Neighbors are Wrestling with God's General Revelation
Vol 2   Thomas K. Johnson: Christian Ethics in Secular Cultures, Vol. 1
Vol 3   David Parker: Discerning the Obedience of Faith: A Short History of the World Evangelical Alliance Theological Commission
Vol 4   Thomas Schirrmacher (Ed.): William Carey: Theologian – Linguist – Social Reformer
Vol 5   Thomas Schirrmacher: Advocate of Love – Martin Bucer as Theologian and Pastor
Vol 6   Thomas Schirrmacher: Culture of Shame / Culture of Guilt
Vol 7   Thomas Schirrmacher: The Koran and the Bible
Vol 8   Thomas Schirrmacher (Ed.): The Humanisation of Slavery in the Old Testament
Vol 9   Jim Harries: New Foundations for Appreciating Africa: Beyond Religious and Secular Deceptions
Vol 10   Thomas Schirrmacher: Missio Dei – God's Missional Nature
Vol 11   Thomas Schirrmacher: Biblical Foundations for 21st Century World Mission
Vol 12   William Wagner, Mark Wagner: Can Evangelicals Truly Change the World? How Seven Philosophical and Religious Movements Are Growing
Vol 13   Thomas Schirrmacher: Modern Fathers
Vol 14   Jim Harries: Jarida juu ya Maisha ya MwAfrika katika huduma ya Ukristo
Vol 15   Peter Lawrence: Fellow Travellers – A Comparative Study on the Identity Formation of Jesus Followers from Jewish, Christian and Muslim Backgrounds in The Holy Land
Vol 16   William Wagner: From Classroom Dummy to University President – Serving God in the Land of Sound of Music
Vol 17   Thomas K. Johnson, David Parker, Thomas Schirrmacher (ed.): In the Name of the Father, Son, and Holy Spirit – Teaching the Trinity from the Creeds to Modern Discussion
Vol 18   Mark Wagner and William Wagner (Ed.): Halfway Up the Mountain
Vol 19   Thomas K. Johnson: The Protester, the Dissident, and the Christian – Essays on Human Rights and Religion
Vol 20   Thomas K. Johnson: Humanitarian Islam, Evangelical Christianity, and the Clash of Civilizations
Vol 21   Thomas K. Johnson: Christian Ethics in Secular Cultures, Vol. 2
Vol 22   Reuben van Rensburg, Thomas Schirrmacher (Ed.): "Be Focused ... Use Common Sense ... Overcome Excuses and Stupidity ..." Festschrift in Honor of Dr. Manfred Waldemar Kohl
Vol 23   John W. Ewing. Goodly Fellowship – A Centenary Tribute to the Life and Work of the World's Evangelical Alliance 1846–1946
Vol 24   Thomas K. Johnson, William S. Barker (Ed.): The Decalogue Project – Disciples from Six Continents Engage God's Ten Commandments
Vol 25   Hannes Wiher: Holistic Mission – An Historical and Theological Study of Its Development, 1966–2011

Hannes Wiher

# Holistic Mission:
## An Historical and Theological Study of Its Development, 1966–2011

WIPF & STOCK · Eugene, Oregon

Wipf and Stock Publishers
199 W 8th Ave, Suite 3
Eugene, OR 97401

Holistic Mission
An Historical and Theological Study of Its Development, 1966-2011
By Wiher, Hannes
Copyright © 2022 Verlag für Kultur und Wissenschaft Culture and Science Publ.
All rights reserved.
Softcover ISBN-13: 978-1-6667-4528-3
Hardcover ISBN-13: 978-1-6667-4529-0
Publication date 4/12/2022
Previously published by Verlag für Kultur und Wissenschaft Culture and Science Publ., 2022

# Contents

Introduction ............................................................................................. 7
    The Meaning of Holistic Mission ................................................................. 7
    Worldview ............................................................................................ 9

## Chapter 1: From Evangelism and Social Action to Holistic Mission: An Historical Perspective ............................................................ 15

    Historical Background and Development of the Debate ....................... 15
    Evangelical Declarations ........................................................................ 18
        Wheaton (1966): Worldwide Mission ................................................ 19
        Berlin (1966): World Evangelism ....................................................... 21
        Frankfurt (1970): The Fundamental Crisis of Mission ...................... 22
        Lausanne (1974): World Evangelization ............................................ 23
        Lausanne (1974): Alternative Declaration on Radical Discipleship.... 26
        Madras and Lima (1979), Pattaya (1980): Social Responsibility.......... 28
        Hoddesdon, London (1980): A Simple Lifestyle ................................ 29
        Grand Rapids (1982): Evangelism and Social Responsibility .............. 30
        Wheaton (1983): The Church in Response to Human Need .............. 31
        Manila (1989): The Whole Gospel to the Whole World ..................... 32
        Oxford (2001): The Micah Network and Integral Mission ................. 35
        Pattaya (2004): Holistic Mission ......................................................... 36
        Cape Town (2010): Love God and Serve the World ........................... 38
        Bangkok (2011): Christian Witness in a Multi-religious World .......... 40
    Conclusion ............................................................................................. 41
    Further Reading ..................................................................................... 42

## Chapter 2: Holistic Mission and the Definition of Mission: A Biblical and Theological Perspective ............................................ 45

    Evangelism and Mission in the Missiological Debate ........................... 45
        Historical Development of the Missiological Debate ........................ 45
        Typological Syntheses of the Missiological Debate ........................... 49
        Multiple Witness ................................................................................. 55

Evangelism and Mission in the Perspective of Worldview ...................... 57
    Development of Worldviews in the Lausanne Movement ................. 58
    Development of Worldviews from Modernity to Late Modernity ..... 59
    Worldviews Underlying the Contextual Theologies of the Global South .................................................................................................. 63

Evangelism and Mission in the Bible ......................................................... 65
    Biblical Terms of the Semantic Domains of Sending and Communication ................................................................................. 66
    Missiological Concepts in the Light of the Bible .................................. 71
    Conceptions of Mission and Salvation ................................................... 75
    Assessment of the Biblical Analysis ....................................................... 77

Conclusion ..................................................................................................... 78

Further Reading ............................................................................................ 78

## Chapter 3: A Holism with Biblical Distinctions ............................... 79

Positive Contribution .................................................................................. 79

Lack of Distinctions and Nuances ............................................................. 79

Evangelism and Social Responsibility ...................................................... 81

Eternal Destiny of Man and Holistic Mission .......................................... 82

Kingdom of God, Mission of God, and Holistic Mission ......................... 83

The Mission of Jesus and of the Disciples ................................................ 84

Eschatology and Holistic Mission .............................................................. 84

Multiple Witness and Holistic Mission ..................................................... 85

Mission as Expression of a Biblical Worldview ....................................... 86

Conclusion ..................................................................................................... 88

## Bibliography ............................................................................................ 89

Evangelical Conference Documents and Declarations ........................... 89

Works Cited ................................................................................................... 91

# Introduction

For the last 50 years, one of the most important discussions in global evangelicalism has concerned the idea of holistic mission, which proposes the integration of verbal evangelism and social engagement within Christian mission. This book examines how key terms such as "evangelism" and "mission" have been understood in the Bible and in contemporary evangelical declarations from 1966 to 2011. It adopts an in-depth approach to the historical, biblical and theological analysis. The main thesis is that the different conceptions of evangelism and mission in general, and that of holistic mission in particular, have their root in the worldview of the various theologians and Christian leaders preparing these statements.

In this introduction, I first present the subject of this reflection—namely, the notion of holistic mission—and the main analytic tool, the notion of worldview. In chapter 1, I undertake a historical analysis of the notions of evangelism and mission in the evangelical declarations from 1966 to 2011. In chapter 2, I evaluate the missiological conceptions of evangelism and mission proposed in the various evangelical declarations in the light of the Bible, so as to derive a biblical understanding of evangelism and mission, which I present in chapter 3.

## The Meaning of Holistic Mission

"Holistic mission has become a household phrase of sorts among evangelical missiologists and missionaries," writes Al Tizon, professor of holistic ministries at Palmer Theological Seminary in the USA.[1] According to René Padilla, "It is now widely accepted that the church's mission is intrinsically holistic."[2] The expression has taken on characteristics of a buzzword, the meaning of which is more or less assumed and which tends to govern assumptions and feelings on a particular topic—in this case, the definition of mission.[3]

---

[1] Al Tizon, "Precursors and Tensions in Holistic Mission: An Historical Overview," in *Holistic Mission: God's Plan for God's People*, eds. Brian Woolnough and Wonsuk Ma (Regnum Edinburgh 2010 Series; Oxford: Regnum, 2010), 61.

[2] C. Rene Padilla, "Holistic Mission," in *Dictionary of Mission Theology: Evangelical Foundations*, eds. John Corrie, Samuel Escobar, Wilbert Shenk (Downers Grove: IVP, 2007), 162.

[3] David J. Hesselgrave, "Holism and Prioritism," in *Paradigms in Conflict: 10 Key Questions in Christian Missions Today* (Grand Rapids: Kregel, 2005), 118.

Since human beings are limited, imperfect and sinful, using the term "holistic" or "integral" may seem pretentious. However, the idea of wholeness and integrality can also mean the totality of the human being as a creature. One can better understand the choice of the expression "integral mission" by noting that the term originated in Latin America (from the Spanish *misión integral*). Another term, "transformation," is often used as a synonym for integral or holistic mission, thereby avoiding allusions to the original Latin American context. At the Wheaton consultation on "The Church in Response to Human Need" in 1983, the Lausanne Movement defined and officially adopted the notion of transformation. The International Fellowship of Evangelical Mission Theologians (INFEMIT), founder of the Oxford Centre for Mission Studies (OCMS), prefers to use this term in its Regnum Books publications and its journal, *Transformation*.[4] Following this logic, INFEMIT was later renamed International Fellowship for Mission as Transformation.

The concept of holistic mission represents at its origin the ideas of the evangelical Latin American theologians who came together in the Latin American Theological Fraternity (FTL), founded by René Padilla and Samuel Escobar in 1970. Both Padilla and Escobar were active in the International Fellowship of Evangelical Students (IFES). They wanted to go beyond the definitions of mission by Western theologians that were limited, as they saw it, to evangelism and church planting, or the "salvation of souls." They viewed these definitions as reductionist tendencies inappropriate for Latin America, a context of poverty and the emergence of liberation theology. David Kirkpatrick summarizes the concept's background:

> The origins of integral mission, then, are found within a revolutionary university context, grounded in the global evangelical student movement, and developed by Latin American thinkers themselves—principally the Ecuadorian theologian C. René Padilla. ... Integral mission themes arose not as a response to developments within the Roman Catholic Church, but as a response to the same political and social stimuli that gave rise to liberation theology.[5]

The concept of holistic mission was thus designed to go beyond the old dichotomy between evangelism and social responsibility that was in-

---

[4] INFEMIT was founded in 1980, OCMS in 1983. Cf. Al Tizon, *Transformation after Lausanne* (Carlisle, UK and Waynesboro, GA: Regnum, 2008).

[5] David C. Kirkpatrick, "C. René Padilla and the Origins of Integral Mission in Post-War Latin America," *Journal of Ecclesiastical History* 67, no. 2 (2016): 351–71; citation on 370–71.

herited from Western theologies of mission. This intention finds its expression in its definition by the Micah Network (2001), strongly influenced by Padilla:

> Integral mission or holistic transformation is the proclamation and demonstration of the gospel. It is not simply that evangelism and social involvement are to be done alongside each other. Rather, in integral mission our proclamation has social consequences as we call people to love and repentance in all areas of life. And our social involvement has evangelistic consequences as we bear witness to the transforming grace of Jesus Christ. ... Justice and justification by faith, worship and political action, the spiritual and the material, personal change and structural change belong together. As in the life of Jesus, being, doing and saying are at the heart of our integral task.[6]

However, the evangelical Latin American theologians did not want to fall into the trap of another reductionism, that of liberation theology, which sees the kingdom of God simply as a material liberation. For Padilla, integral mission involves "engagement in the world, mission to political life (including the prophetic, the servant and the evangelistic tasks), action and prayer at the level of the local church, church growth, and Christian presence."[7]

Padilla's quotation illustrates clearly the Latin American theologians' approach to the human situation. It stands in opposition to the conceptions of Western theologians who had, according to the Latin Americans, a reductionist view of mission. This perspective corresponds well to my thesis that the different approaches to mission in general, and to holistic mission in particular, have their root in the theologians' differing worldviews. In the next section, I present briefly the concept of worldview, an important analytic tool in this study.

## Worldview

Introduced into the field of philosophy by Immanuel Kant in 1790,[8] the concept of worldview (*Weltanschauung*) subsequently imposed itself on

---

[6] "Micah Network Declaration on Integral Mission (2001)," https://live-micah-global.pantheonsite.io/wp-content/uploads/2020/10/integral_mission_declaration_en.pdf.

[7] C. René Padilla, "Global Partnership and Integral Mission," in *Mission in Context: Explorations Inspired by J. Andrew Kirk*, eds. John Corrie and Cathy Ross (Farnham: Ashgate, 2012), 58.

[8] Immanuel Kant, *Critique of the Power of Judgment*, ed. and trans. Paul Guyer (1790; Cambridge: Cambridge University Press, 2008), I, 2, § 26.

other sciences. It entered the world of the natural sciences through the notion of "tacit dimension" coined by Michael Polanyi, describing the logic and relational network underlying every scientific analysis.[9] In the social sciences, the concept received a warm welcome; in cultural anthropology, for example, Franz Boas found that all cultures have underlying patterns that give coherence to their diverse cultural traits.[10]

According to philosopher David Naugle, a worldview is "a system of narrative signs that establishes a powerful framework within which people think (reason), interpret (hermeneutics), and know (epistemology)."[11] This definition shows the cultural influence on logic, hermeneutics, and epistemology. In the same vein but in another discipline, cultural anthropologist Clifford Geertz defines worldview as the way we perceive ourselves and the world around us. It is the image that the members of a culture have in common on the way things really are, a perception of nature, self and society.[12] Worldviews are thus "glasses" through which we perceive and conceive ourselves and the world. In a functionalist perspective, we can understand worldview as a set of interpretations of the world, society, and ourselves in order to answer questions and solve problems.[13] For Paul Hiebert, worldviews provide "the foundational cognitive, affective, and evaluative assumptions and frameworks a group of people makes about the nature of reality which they use to order their lives."[14] Worldview is thus a strategy to understand ourselves and the world and to manage life.

Naugle observes that the evangelical community has widely adopted the concept of worldview: "In the entire history of 'worldview', no single philosophic school or religious community has given more sustained attention to or taken more advantage of this concept than Protestant evangelicals."[15] The reason for this, according to Carl Henry, is that it offers the

---

[9] Michael Polanyi, *The Tacit Dimension* (Garden City, NY: Doubleday, 1966); cf. also Polanyi, *Personal Knowledge: Towards a Post-Critical Philosophy* (Chicago: University of Chicago Press, 1958).

[10] Cf. David K. Naugle, *Worldview: The History of a Concept* (Grand Rapids: Eerdmans, 2001), 209-52; Paul G. Hiebert, *Transforming Worldviews: An Anthropological Understanding of How People Change* (Grand Rapids: Baker, 2008), 15-25.

[11] Naugle, *Worldview*, xix; cf. a similar formulation on p. 253 and the explanation on pp. 291-330.

[12] Clifford Geertz, *The Interpretation of Cultures* (New York: Basic Books, 1973).

[13] Cf. the analogous definition of culture by Lothar Käser, "Culture as a Strategy," in *Foreign Cultures: An Introduction to Ethnology* (Nürnberg: VTR, 2014), 36f.

[14] Hiebert, *Transforming Worldviews*, 15, 25.

[15] Naugle, *Worldview*, 31.

possibility of an explanation of the totality of reality and "demonstrates the rational coherence of the Biblical revelation."[16] Naugle goes even further:

> Conceiving of Christianity as a worldview has been one of the most significant developments in the recent history of the church. ... The explanatory power, intellectual coherence, and pragmatic effectiveness of the Christian worldview not only make it exceedingly relevant for believers personally, but also establish a solid foundation for vigorous cultural and academic engagement.[17]

However, the general notion of worldview, being ill-defined and fuzzy, has been abandoned by many scholars outside of Protestant evangelicalism. In this book, I take the opposite approach by operationalizing worldview. In the following discussion on the definition of evangelism and mission, I will include the cosmological, soteriological, elenctic[18] and temporal dimensions of worldview. I thus propose an operationalizing model for every dimension. For the cosmological dimension, I introduce the *stratigraphic model of creation*. This model answers the worldview question: Where are we? It categorizes worldview according to the creational strata: spiritual beings, humans, animals, plants, matter. The model includes four ideal types of worldview: a holistic, Hebrew, dichotomizing and secular worldview. I present them schematically in Table 1.[19]

The holistic worldview includes all the strata of the creational order, visible and invisible, i.e. all aspects of the human condition. The Hebrew worldview tends towards a holistic worldview but places God the Creator in opposition to the created universe. On the other hand, the dichotomizing worldview distinguishes and separates the visible and invisible aspects of the universe. It excludes the "middle," the sphere that entails spiritual beings influencing the well-being or ill-being of humans according to the

---

[16] Carl F. H. Henry, "Fortunes of the Christian World View," *Trinity Journal* 19 (1998): 163.
[17] Naugle, *Worldview*, 4–5.
[18] Elenctics (from the Greek *elenghō*, "convict," cf. Jn 16:8) is the study of the conscience. It is an important part of the study of evangelism, where the question of the Holy Spirit's influence on the conscience is central. Cf. Johan H. Bavinck, "Elenctics," in *An Introduction to the Science of Missions* (Philadelphia: Presbyterian and Reformed, 1960), 221–72.
[19] The model has been adapted from Paul G. Hiebert, *Anthropological Insights for Missionaries* (Grand Rapids: Baker, 1985), 158. For a more detailed discussion of the stratigraphic model of creation, see Hannes Wiher, "Worldview and Identity across Conversion," *Evangelical Review of Theology* 38, no. 4 (2014): 308–10.

animist worldview.[20] The secular worldview does not consider the invisible aspects of the universe.

Table 1: Stratigraphic Model of Creation

| Holistic Worldview | Hebrew Worldview | Dichotomizing Worldview | Secular Worldview |
|---|---|---|---|
|  | God |  | Invisible aspect excluded |
| Supreme Being |  | Spirit | |
| Ancestors Spirits | Angels Spirits | "Excluded Middle" | |
| Humans | Humans | Humans | Humans |
| Animals | Animals | Animals | Animals |
| Plants | Plants | Plants | Plants |
| Matter | Matter | Matter | Matter |

A second model to operationalize worldview consists of the *five soteriological concepts*: God, man, evil, sin, and salvation. They build together a worldview, biblical or other. They answer the following typical worldview questions: Where do we come from? What has gone wrong? What is the solution? During the discipleship process, before and after conversion, we have to work on them and transform a cultural worldview into a biblical worldview. If these transformative Bible studies are not part of the discipleship process, people's worldviews will not change.[21] John Calvin's stay at Geneva provides a significant example: during a period of just 18 years, the reformer preached between 2,500 and 5,000 sermons across the whole Bible. In this way, he transformed the worldview of the inhabitants of Geneva. For these five concepts, the soteriological dimensions of worldview, I refer the reader to their presentations in theological textbooks. In the following discussion, I will especially discuss the dichotomizing and holistic conceptions of salvation.

---

[20] Paul G. Hiebert, "The Flaw of the Excluded Middle," *Missiology: An International Review* 10, no. 1 (1982): 35–47; cf. also Paul G. Hiebert, Daniel R. Shaw, Tite Tiénou, "Split-Level Christianity," in *Understanding Folk Religion: A Christian Response to Popular Beliefs and Practices* (Grand Rapids: Baker, 1999), 89–91.

[21] Wiher, "Worldview and Identity across Conversion."

Whereas the first two models represent the cognitive aspects of worldview, the model of *conscience orientation* integrates the affective and evaluative aspects in the worldview approach and reaches in this way the deepest layers of personality, culture, and religion. It is a combined theological, psychological, and anthropological model that is particularly fertile. The conscience is a useful model because this notion is important in both the Bible and cultural anthropology. In the Bible, the conscience refers to the path from sin through forgiveness to salvation and thus deals with the core of the biblical message. In cultural anthropology, some authors classify the cultures on the basis of their shame or guilt orientation, feelings that are presented in the Bible as possible expressions of sin, whether relationally or legally. The relational worldview is linked with a holistic conception of things, and thus with a holistic worldview. On the other hand, the legal conscience orientation joins generally fragmented conceptions of creation, dichotomizing and secular worldviews. Of course, the conscience orientations do not represent reality; they are Weberian ideal types like all models. Every person and culture is a mix of the two orientations, situated somewhere on the spectrum between the two ideal types.[22]

The model of conscience orientation includes two approaches to the notion of *time*, our fourth model. Rules-centered persons manage their lives with their agenda and want to be punctual. Conversely, relational persons have little consideration for time and are oriented toward persons, relations, and events. Ecclesiastes 3:1–8 represents an event orientation typical of relational cultures. This fourth model of worldview introduces a supplementary aspect of time, namely a *past or future orientation*. This aspect asks questions such as "Where do we come from?" and "Where are we going?" It explains why some persons and cultures do or do not value traditions or plan ahead of time with difficulty or ease. This model will be of particular importance when we discuss the link between the conception of mission and eschatology in chapter 3.[23]

I will add a remark concerning the notion of *biblical worldview*. It is not limited to the Hebrew worldview as presented in the stratigraphic model of creation, but is defined by a certain configuration of the four models

---

[22] Hannes Wiher, *Shame and Guilt: A Key to Cross-Cultural Ministry* (Bonn: Culture and Science Publications, 2003).

[23] Cf. Sherwood G. Lingenfelter and Marvin K. Mayers, "Tensions about Time" and "Tensions Associated with Handling Crises," in *Ministering Cross-Culturally. An Incarnational Model for Personal Relationships* (Grand Rapids: Baker Academic, 1986, 2003), 37–50, 65–76.

together. The ideal type of the Hebrew worldview in the stratigraphic model thus represents only one aspect of a biblical worldview. With regard to this model, the Bible presents a worldview that sets the holistic and the dichotomizing approaches in tension. It introduces several important dichotomies, such as between the Creator and creation, body and "soul/spirit," light and darkness, among others. In the Old Testament, over more than a thousand years, different expressions of the biblical worldview are presented. In the New Testament, the Jewish authors integrate Greek dichotomizing notions to a different degree in their worldview. We will not be able to solve the problem of the multiplicity of biblical worldviews. I prefer to define the biblical worldview (and others) by the four models presented: the stratigraphic model of creation, the five soteriological concepts, conscience orientation, and the orientations of time. This biblical worldview includes, of course, the grounding of the Old Testament and its differentiation in the New Testament.[24]

In the following chapter, I will present the missiological debates on evangelism and mission and discuss their different conceptions on the basis of the relevant evangelical declarations issued from 1966 to 2011.

---

[24] For a more detailed discussion of worldview in general and a biblical worldview in particular, see Wiher, "Worldview and Identity across Conversion," 308–16.

# CHAPTER I

# From Evangelism and Social Action to Holistic Mission: An Historical Perspective

In this chapter, I reflect on the debate about the definition of mission in the evangelical movement during the second half of the twentieth century. From an emphasis on the relationship between evangelism and social responsibility, the debate developed toward the concept of holistic mission. We will study the relevant evangelical declarations between 1966 and 2011, especially those of the Lausanne Movement, in relation to the underlying worldview. As stated above, my main thesis is that the worldview of each theologian influences the different approaches to the definition of mission. We will concentrate on the intra-evangelical debate, with some referrals to the broader ecumenical debate.

As worldview is a philosophical concept adopted by other sciences, our approach will be interdisciplinary with a particular emphasis on historical and theological analysis. After a short presentation of the historical background of the debate, I will analyze the evangelical declarations. This historical reflection will show the development of the missiological debate and the difficulties involved in defining evangelism and mission.

## Historical Background and Development of the Debate

Following Jesus' example, Catholic and Protestant missionaries of all time periods of church history tried to meet the needs of the populations among whom they served. They viewed human beings and their needs as a whole. For them, the issue of the dichotomizing tension between evangelism and social action did not yet exist. The revivals of the eighteenth and nineteenth centuries, which gave birth to the Protestant missionary movement, did not change their holistic approach.

During the nineteenth century, a dichotomy appeared as a logical consequence of two centuries of Enlightenment philosophy and an increasingly secular worldview. The "Social Gospel" current, which valued material concerns more highly than the spiritual dimension, became prominent. Meanwhile, to emphasize the spiritual side of world mission, Protestant mission societies organized a missionary conference in Edinburgh in 1910. According to Kenneth Latourette, it "was the cradle of the ecumenical movement."[25] The ecumenical movement adopted the theological positions of the Social Gospel, insisting on the socio-political aspects of the Christian message. In reaction to the Social Gospel, the Fundamentalist movement became more strident, calling people back to the basic Christian doctrines. Following it, the evangelical current gave priority to the proclamation of the gospel at the expense of social action.

However, in many evangelical missionary societies, social involvement continued just as during the nineteenth century, introducing a contradiction between theological discourse and daily missionary practice.[26] Samuel Escobar and John Driver describe the missionaries' commitment alongside the underprivileged in this way:

> The missionaries were constantly the protectors of native peoples against exploitation and injustice by government and commercial companies. ... They played a very important part in the abolishing of forced labor in the Congo. They resisted blackbirding in the South Pacific. They fought fiercely for human rights in combating opium, foot-binding, and exposure of girl babies in China. They waged war against widow-burning, infanticide, and temple prostitution in India, and above all broke the social and economic slavery of the caste system for the low and outcaste peoples.[27]

This is why David Moberg calls the retreat by evangelicals from social action and society the "great reversal."[28] The evangelical current manifests itself during the first half of the twentieth century as a "Fundamentalist" reaction to the Social Gospel.

---

[25] Kenneth S. Latourette, "Ecumenical Bearings of the Missionary Movement and the International Missionary Council," in *A History of the Ecumenical Movement, vol. 1: 1517-1948*, ed. Ruth Rouse and Stephen C. Neill (Geneva: World Council of Churches, 1993), 362.

[26] Al Tizon, "Precursors and Tensions in Holistic Mission: An Historical Overview," in *Holistic Mission: God's Plan for God's People*, ed. Brian Woolnough and Wonsuk Ma (Regnum Edinburgh 2010 Series; Oxford: Regnum, 2010), 66.

[27] Samuel Escobar and John Driver, *Christian Mission and Social Justice* (Scottdale, PA: Herald, 1978), 8f.

[28] David O. Moberg, *The Great Reversal: Evangelism versus Social Concern* (Philadelphia and New York: Lippincott, 1972), 30-34, expanding on Timothy L. Smith, "Recent Historical Perspectives of the Evangelical Tradition," in *Christian Relief and Development: Developing Workers for Effective Ministry*, ed. Edgar J. Elliston (Dallas: Word, 1989), 11, 30, and George M. Marsden, *Fundamentalism and American Culture. The Shaping of Twentieth Century Evangelicalism, 1870-1925* (New York and Oxford: Oxford University Press, 1980), 85.

The main factors in the division between evangelicals and ecumenicals were, according to Billy Graham, the passage from an individualist to a communitarian approach to conversion and from evangelism to social action. For him, the control of mission activity by church dignitaries was the principal cause of the absence of zeal for world evangelism. Whereas the ecumenical current held theological debates without important missionary activities, the evangelical current maintained an intense missionary activism.[29]

After World War II, in the 1950s and 1960s, the "neo-evangelical" and "post-fundamentalist" movement appeared. It was an attempt to balance fundamentalist theology, represented by Billy Graham, Harold Ockenga, Harold Lindsell, and Carl F. H. Henry. Henry remarked, "By revolting against the Social Gospel, Fundamentalism has revolted also against the Christian social imperative."[30] Later, he referred to the position that emphasized "only evangelism" as "fundamentalist reductionism."[31] According to Joel Carpenter, the neo-evangelicals had to virtually "reinvent" an evangelical theology of missions.[32] The declaration of the missionary congress at Wheaton (1966) sums up well the development of the concept of mission:

> Whereas evangelicals in the eighteenth and nineteenth centuries led in social concern, in the twentieth century many lost the biblical perspective and limited themselves only to preaching a gospel of individual salvation without sufficient involvement in their social and community responsibilities. When theological liberalism and humanism invaded historic Protestant churches and proclaimed a "social gospel," the conviction grew among evangelicals that an antithesis existed between social involvement and gospel witness. Today, however, evangelicals are increasingly convinced that they must involve themselves in the great social problems men are facing. They are concerned for the needs of the whole man, because of their Lord's example, His constraining love, their identity with the human race, and the challenge of their evangelical heritage.[33]

---

[29] Billy Graham, "Why Lausanne?" in *Let the Earth Hear His Voice: Official Reference Volume, Papers and Responses*, International Congress on World Evangelization Lausanne, ed. James D. Douglas (Minneapolis: World Wide Publications, 1975), 26.

[30] Carl F. H. Henry, *The Uneasy Conscience of Modern Fundamentalism* (Grand Rapids: Eerdmans, 1947), 32.

[31] Carl F. H. Henry, *Evangelical Responsibility in Contemporary Theology* (Grand Rapids: Eerdmans, 1957), 33.

[32] Joel Carpenter and Wilbert Shenk, *Earthen Vessels: American Evangelicals and Foreign Missions 1880-1980* (Grand Rapids: Eerdmans, 1990), 131.

[33] "Wheaton Declaration," *International Review of Mission* 55, no. 220 (1966): 473.

A typical example for the holistic approach of evangelicals in the eighteenth century is William Carey (1761–1834), the "father of modern missions." Carey studied the languages and cultures of India, wrote dictionaries and encyclopedias, translated the Bible, preached the gospel, started schools, hospitals, agricultural projects and humanitarian initiatives, planted churches, and trained pastors. He was also involved in the interdiction of the burning of widows and infanticide in India. However, theologically he saw himself as a missionary of Christ for the conversion of Indians and church planting in India.[34]

Summing up the historical process in relation to the definition of mission, James Scherer observes a development from an orientation toward individual conversion in the nineteenth century, via an ecclesiocentric orientation in the first half of the twentieth century, to a broader definition of a kingdom-of-God perspective during the second half of the twentieth century.[35]

## Evangelical Declarations

In the 1960s, the conviction ripened among leaders of the evangelical movement that the moment for the creation of a separate platform of evangelical reflection has come. In 1974, a gathering of evangelicals led to the creation of the Lausanne Movement, which organized several congresses on world evangelism that issued statements on mission. These declarations prepared the ground for a more robust perspective on missions in the evangelical movement. In this section, I present the development of the concepts of evangelism and mission through the lens of these evangelical declarations. I concentrate on the debates around the definition of evangelism and mission, methods, and underlying worldviews.

Before the first Lausanne congress in 1974 (Lausanne I), the evangelicals organized three preparatory congresses: the Wheaton Congress in 1966 on "the Church's worldwide mission," the Congress on World Evangelism in Berlin in the same year, and a congress on "the fundamental

---

[34] Cf. also the title of William Carey's pamphlet: "An Enquiry into the Obligations of Christians to Use Means for the Conversion of the Heathens" (1792).

[35] James A. Scherer, *Gospel, Church and Kingdom: Comparative Studies in World Mission Theology* (Minneapolis: Augsburg, 1987), 320. See also the summaries in David J. Bosch, "The Two Mandates," in *Transforming Mission: Paradigm Shifts in Theology of Mission* (Maryknoll: Orbis, 1991), 403–8; David J. Hesselgrave, "The Kingdom of God and the Church of Christ," in *Paradigms in Conflict*, 317–26; Tizon, "Precursors and Tensions in Holistic Mission," 61–75; Henning Wrogemann, *Intercultural Theology*, vol. 2: *Theologies of Mission* (Downers Grove: IVP Academic, 2018), 59–115.

crisis of mission" in Frankfurt in 1970. After Lausanne I (1974), the organized two follow-up congresses—Manila (1989), known as Lausanne II, and Cape Town (2010) or Lausanne III—along with about fifty consultations. I concentrate here on those consultations that reflected on the definition of mission and the relationship between evangelism and social responsibility.[36]

During this period, Christianity became a world movement. In 1910, 81 percent of Christians lived in the Global North (66 percent Europeans, and 15 percent North Americans) and only 19 percent in the Global South, by 2010 62 percent of all Christians were living in the Global South. Africa in 2010 was a Christian-majority continent and the home of 22 percent of Christians worldwide. There thus occurred what Andrew Walls calls Christianity's "transfer of the center of gravity."[37] This transfer has, of course, implications for the missionary movement: if in 1910, missions reached "from the West to the rest," in 2010 missionaries were going "from everywhere to everywhere." At the ecumenical missionary conference in Mexico in 1963, the slogan was "mission in six continents."

This transfer also has had implications for the way of conceiving and doing theology. Generally speaking, whereas Western theologians conceived of their theology on the basis of a dichotomizing worldview, the theologians of the Global South based their theologizing on a holistic worldview. I will point out this distinction when discussing the various declarations below.

## Wheaton (1966): Worldwide Mission

In April 1966, a thousand participants from more than seventy countries attended a missionary congress in Wheaton (USA), initiated by Billy Graham and his association. Its objective was "to engage in serious study of the Church's worldwide mission."[38] Notably, it still used the term "mission" to denote world evangelism. This mission was considered central to

---

[36] For the consultations and their reports, see the Lausanne Occasional Papers on the website of the Lausanne Movement, www.lausanne.org.

[37] Andrew F. Walls, "From Christendom to World Christianity: Missions and the Demographic Transformation of the Church," in idem, *The Cross-Cultural Process in Christian History* (Maryknoll: Orbis, 2002), 49–71, particularly 58; Walls, "Christian Mission in a Five-Hundred-Year Context," in *Mission in the 21st Century: Exploring the Five Marks of Global Mission*, ed. Andrew F. Walls and Cathy Ross (London: Darton, Longman & Todd, 2008), 193–204.

[38] "Wheaton Declaration," 458. From here on, we indicate the references to the declarations between parentheses in the text.

evangelicals: "We regard as crucial the 'evangelistic mandate.' ... This is the supreme task of the Church" (461–62).

Right at the beginning, the declaration includes a confession of neglect of relevant evangelism:

> We have sinned grievously. We are guilty of an unscriptural isolation from the world that too often keeps us from honestly facing and coping with its concerns. In our Christian service, we depend too much on promotion and publicity, too little on importunate prayer and the Holy Spirit. We frequently fail to communicate the Gospel in a relevant, winsome fashion (460).

The participants perceived themselves as countering the ecumenical movement and its liberal tendencies:

> Contemporary Protestant movements that boldly contend for the non-existence of the Gospel revealed by God, that propagate a neo-universalism denying eternal condemnation, that substitute inter-church reconciling service for aggressive evangelism, that blur the biblical distinction between Church and Mission, between Romanism and Protestantism, and that create ecclesiastical organizations moving in the direction of a worldwide religious monopoly, likewise demand a careful assessment and response (461).

The definition of the gospel given here is the Gospel restricted to the person of Jesus Christ: "The Gospel concerns the God-man, Jesus of Nazareth" (462). The text affirms the priority of preaching this gospel: "The Gospel must be preached in our generation to the peoples of every tribe, tongue, and nation" (461).

Concerning social action, the declaration points to the Bible to guide evangelicals in maintaining the priority of gospel preaching and of individual salvation:

> Evangelicals look to the Scriptures for guidance as to what they should do, and how far they should go in expressing this social concern, without minimizing the priority of preaching the Gospel of individual salvation. The Old Testament manifests God's concern for social justice (Micah 6:8). Our Lord, by precept and example, stressed the importance of ministering to the physical and social, as well as spiritual needs of men (Matt. 5–9). His dealings with the Samaritans involved Him in racial and social issues (Luke 9:51–56; John 4:1–30; Luke 10:25–37). His disciples followed His example (Gal. 2:10; Col. 3:11; James 1:27; 2:9–11). They taught and respected the role of government in promoting civil justice (e.g. Romans 13 and 1 Peter 2). The two great commandments are: "Love the Lord thy God ... and thy neighbour as thyself" (Mark 12:29–31) (473–74).

For the first time in the evangelical movement, the declaration includes a call to a greater involvement in social action:

> We therefore declare: That we reaffirm unreservedly the primacy of preaching the Gospel to every creature and we will demonstrate anew God's concern for social justice and human welfare; That evangelical social action will include, wherever possible, a verbal witness to Jesus Christ; ... That when Christian institutions no longer fulfil their distinctively evangelical functions they should be relinquished (474).

The Wheaton Declaration displays a remarkable theological balance, underscoring the importance of social action while also affirming the importance and priority of preaching the gospel at every moment. According to René Padilla, the large number of participants from the Global South was the reason for the new preoccupation for social action.[39]

## Berlin (1966): World Evangelism

In October 1966, evangelicals organized a second preparatory congress, this time in Europe: the World Congress on Evangelism in Berlin. It gathered more than a thousand evangelicals from over a hundred countries. It was again an initiative of the Billy Graham Evangelistic Association together with *Christianity Today*, a journal founded in 1956 by Billy Graham as an evangelical alternative to *The Christian Century*, the main journal of American Protestantism. In his introductory address, Billy Graham felt the need to define evangelism explicitly and to affirm its importance:

> Evangelism consists of offering Jesus Christ in the power of the Holy Spirit in a way that men put their trust in God, accept him as their Savior and serve him as their King in the community of his Church. ... I am convinced if the Church went back to its main task of proclaiming the Gospel and getting people converted to Christ, it would have a far greater impact on the social, moral and psychological needs of men than any other thing it could possibly do.[40]

During this same congress, John Stott excluded social action from the mission of the Church in one of his three studies on the Great Commission: "The commission of the Church, therefore, is not to reform society, but to preach the

---

[39] C. Rene Padilla, "Evangelism and Social Responsibility: From Wheaton '66 to Wheaton '83," *Transformation* 2, no. 3 (1985): 27–34, particularly 28.

[40] Billy Graham, "Why Berlin 1966?" in *One Race, One Gospel, One Task: World Congress on Evangelism, Berlin 1966*, vol. 1, ed. Carl F. H. Henry and W. Stanley Mooneyham (Minneapolis: World Wide Publications, 1967), 25, 28.

gospel. ... The primary task of the members of Christ's Church is to be gospel heralds, not social reformers. ... Again, the commission of the Church is not to heal the sick, but to preach the gospel."[41] Interestingly, Stott was defending a more restricted concept of mission than that of the Wheaton Declaration.

## Frankfurt (1970): The Fundamental Crisis of Mission

The third preparatory congress of Lausanne I on "the fundamental crisis of mission" took place in Frankfurt in 1970. Its initiator was the German Lutheran missiologist Peter Beyerhaus, professor of missiology at Tübingen and defender of the evangelical cause in the ecumenical movement.[42] Its content was similar to that of the Berlin congress.

Summing up the preparatory congresses to Lausanne I, we can see that none of them devoted much attention to the social responsibility of the Christian, but that all concentrated on world evangelism. According to Efiong Utuk, they constituted basically the beginning of "a movement against the World Council of Churches."[43] Perhaps this motive that made the gathering of the evangelical movement possible in the first place. Al Tizon perceived three groups among the evangelicals during this period preceding Lausanne I: (1) the fundamentalists who maintained the priority of evangelism at the expense of social responsibility, (2) the neo-evangelicals who defended a return to a historical view of social involvement while maintaining the priority of evangelism, and (3) the radical evangelicals who promoted a sociopolitical commitment as an integral part of the gospel.[44] On the other hand, Peter Beyerhaus and David Bosch discerned six branches in the evangelical movement. Along with the three mentioned by Tizon, they distinguished the Pentecostals and Charismatics, the evangelicals in the Protestant denominations, and the evangelicals who sympathized with the ecumenical movement.[45] The evangelical movement was thus very diverse, adopting a variety of theological positions.

---

[41] John Stott, "The Great Commission," in *One Race, One Gospel, One Task*, 37.

[42] "Frankfurt Declaration on the Fundamental Crisis of Mission," *Christianity Today* June 19 (1970): 3–6. For a detailed discussion of the congress and the declaration, see Peter Beyerhaus, *Krise und Neuaufbruch der Weltmission* (Bad Liebenzell, VLM, 1987), 1–80.

[43] Efiong S. Utuk, "From Wheaton to Lausanne," in *New Directions in Mission and Evangelization*, vol. 2: *Theological Foundations*, ed. James A. Scherer and Stephen B. Bevans (Maryknoll, NY: Orbis, 1994), 101.

[44] Tizon, "Precursors and Tensions in Holistic Mission," 65.

[45] David Bosch, *Witness to the World: The Christian Mission in Theological Perspective* (Atlanta: John Knox Press, London: Marshall, Morgan & Scott, 1980), 30.

## Lausanne (1974): World Evangelization

In view of this internal diversity, we can understand the birth of the Lausanne movement in the light of theological positions adopted by the ecumenical movement. Whereas the fourth General Assembly of the World Council of Churches (WCC) at Uppsala in 1968 decided to support rebel movements, and whereas the Commission for World Mission and Evangelism conference at Bangkok in 1973 spoke of "humanization of the world" and of "salvation today," the evangelicals wanted to reflect more profoundly on world evangelism.[46] Donald McGavran's call at Uppsala to include the two billion unevangelized people in the reflections of the General Assembly remained without echo.[47] Roger Hedlund remarked, "Two theologies—two ideologies—are in conflict ... on one side the advocates of mission as humanization, on the other ... evangelism of lost souls."[48]

After three preparatory gatherings of the evangelicals, the moment for the creation of a separate evangelical movement had come. Billy Graham and his association together with John Stott, an Anglican evangelical, convened the first congress for world evangelization at Lausanne in 1974, with more than four thousand Christians from around the world participating. Stott presided at the formulation of the Lausanne Covenant. Note that this was not a congress for world mission, but for world evangelization. The term "evangelization" seemed preferable to the organizers because it was supposed to be less ambiguous and less offensive.[49]

At Lausanne, the evangelical movement maintained the priority given to evangelism at Wheaton. Paragraph 6 of the Lausanne covenant notes, "In the Church's mission of sacrificial service evangelism is primary." However, in relation to his position at the Berlin congress, John Stott had evolved in his conception: he no longer identified mission with evangelism, but now considered mission is a broader notion than evangelism. At

---

[46] Peter Beyerhaus, "Mission and Humanization," *International Review of Mission* 60, no. 237 (1971): 11–24; Wrogemann, *Intercultural Theology*, vol. 2: *Theologies of Mission*, 107–12.

[47] Later published in Donald McGavran, "Missiology Faces the Lion," *Missiology* 17, no. 3 (1989): 335–56.

[48] Roger Hedlund, *Roots of the Great Debate in Mission* (Bangalore, India: Theological Book Trust, 1997), 229.

[49] Cf. Ralph Winter, "The Highest Priority: Cross-Cultural Evangelism," in Douglas, *Let the Earth Hear His Voice*, 213–225. For a retrospective view on the differential meanings of mission, evangelism, and evangelization in the Lausanne Movement, cf. Tormod Engelsviken, "Mission, Evangelism and Evangelization: From the Perspective of the Lausanne Movement," *International Review of Mission* 96 (2007): 204–9.

Berlin, Stott had met theologians from the Global South with a holistic perspective on mission, notably Samuel Escobar and René Padilla from Latin America. Confronted with massive poverty in their context, they included the Christian response to the needs of the poor populations within their concept of mission. In *Christian Mission in the Modern World* (1977), published shortly after Lausanne I, Stott defined mission more precisely as "properly a comprehensive word, embracing everything which God sends his people into the world to do. It therefore includes evangelism and social responsibility, since both are authentic expressions of the love which longs to serve man in his need."[50]

From a position that considered evangelism and mission as synonymous, Stott had moved to a narrower definition of evangelism and a broad view of mission. Later on, Stott would define mission as the missionary mandate added to the double commandment of love of God and neighbor. His formula was *Great Commission plus Great Commandment*.

In consequence, paragraph 4 of the Lausanne Covenant,[51] entitled "The Nature of Evangelism," defines evangelism within a narrow perspective geared to the proclamation of the gospel:

> To evangelize is to spread the good news that Jesus Christ died for our sins and was raised from the dead according to the Scriptures, and that as the reigning Lord he now offers the forgiveness of sins and the liberating gifts of the Spirit to all who repent and believe. Our Christian presence in the world is indispensable to evangelism, and so is that kind of dialogue whose purpose is to listen sensitively in order to understand. But evangelism itself is the proclamation of the historical, biblical Christ as Savior and Lord, with a view to persuading people to come to him personally and so be reconciled to God.

Although, in the wording of this passage, the notion of the gospel was restricted to the person of Jesus Christ and evangelism to proclamation and persuasion, at the same time the notion of evangelism was opened to the two notions of presence and dialogue promoted by the ecumenical movement. Paragraph 5 then defines social responsibility:

> We affirm that God is both the Creator and the Judge of all people. We therefore should share his concern for justice and reconciliation throughout human society and for the liberation of men and women from every

---

[50] John Stott, *Christian Mission in the Modern World* (London: Falcon, 1975; Downers Grove: IVP, 2013), 55.

[51] "The Lausanne Covenant," https://www.lausanne.org/content/covenant/lausanne-covenant.

kind of oppression. Because men and women are made in the image of God, every person, regardless of race, religion, colour, culture, class, sex or age, has an intrinsic dignity because of which he or she should be respected and served, not exploited. Here too we express penitence both for our neglect and for having sometimes regarded evangelism and social concern as mutually exclusive. Although reconciliation with other people is not reconciliation with God, nor is social action evangelism, nor is political liberation salvation, nevertheless we affirm that evangelism and socio-political involvement are both part of our Christian duty. For both are necessary expressions of our doctrines of God and man, our love for our neighbour and our obedience to Jesus Christ. ... The salvation we claim should be transforming us in the totality of our personal and social responsibilities. Faith without works is dead.

By specifying that "social action [is not] evangelism, nor is political liberation salvation," the Lausanne Covenant differentiates itself from both liberal theology and liberation theology. By affirming that "in the Church's mission of sacrificial service evangelism is primary" (§ 6), the text confirms Billy Graham's emphasis on evangelism. Despite the fact that the two are distinct, "evangelism and socio-political involvement are both part of our Christian duty" and are "necessary expressions of ... our love for our neighbor" (§ 5). As defined in Stott's book, *Christian Mission in the Modern World*, "mission ... is properly a comprehensive word, embracing everything which God sends his people into the world to do."[52] According to his presentation at the congress, the double commandment of love of God and neighbor is a sufficient justification for social action (Mt 22:37-39). Based on the foundation of the doctrines of God, man and creation, "love does not need to justify itself."[53]

How should we conceive of the relationship between evangelism and social action? The Lausanne Covenant leaves this issue unresolved, despite the hope that Billy Graham formulated in his opening speech: "I trust we can state ... the relationship between evangelism and social responsibility ... [is a question that] disturbs many believers. Perhaps Lausanne can help to clarify it."[54] We must wait for the consultation at Grand Rapids in 1982 to see more precision on this issue.[55]

---

[52] Stott, *Christian Mission in the Modern World*, 55.
[53] John Stott, "Biblical Basis of Evangelism," in Douglas, *Let the Earth Hear His Voice*, 68.
[54] Graham, "Why Lausanne?" 34.
[55] For an evaluation of the Lausanne congress, cf. John Stott, *The Lausanne Covenant: An Exposition and Commentary* (Minneapolis: World Wide Publications, 1975); John Stott, "Significance of Lausanne," *International Review of Mission* 64, no. 255 (1975): 288–94.

According to a retrospective evaluation by Christopher Wright thirty-five years later, the Lausanne Covenant has had great influence:

> This text allows the understanding of the different aspects of mission. It insists on the parallel necessities of evangelism and social action. The Covenant reminds us of the necessity to teach mission and to train oneself in mission by considering the cultural context, and it reflects the integral dimension of Biblical teaching. This Covenant has permitted to unite evangelical Christians around a core of common convictions and faith relative to mission.[56]

Note the holistic tendency of Wright's terminology and evaluation. For missiologist Henning Wrogemann, the Lausanne Covenant "constitutes the most significant declaration of evangelical mission theology."[57] For Jacques Matthey, former general secretary of the WCC Evangelism and Mission Commission, the creation of a separate evangelical structure meant a third rupture between the ecumenical and evangelical movement. For him, the first rupture was the evangelicals' absence from the International Missionary Council (IMC) in 1921, and the second was the refusal by certain evangelical mission societies to become part of the WCC when the IMC was incorporated into the WCC in 1961.[58]

## Lausanne (1974): Alternative Declaration on Radical Discipleship

A group of about six hundred participants at the Lausanne Congress, mainly from the Global South but also including some from North America and Europe, was not fully satisfied with some of the presentations and discussions around the Lausanne Covenant edited under the presidency of John Stott. At the initiative of Samuel Escobar and René Padilla, this group formulated an alternative declaration entitled "Theological Implications of Radical Discipleship." It stimulated very vivid and controversial reactions. John Stott, however, signed it. With his support, it was included in the acts of the congress.[59] Probably because of this title and the group's

---

[56] Christopher Wright, "Love God, Serve the World," *Christianity Today* September (2010): 15.
[57] Wrogemann, *Intercultural Theology*, vol. 2: *Theologies of Mission*, 117.
[58] Jacques Matthey, "Édimbourg 1910 et son approche de la relation entre mission et unité," *Histoire et missions chrétiennes* no. 13 (2010): 71–92, citation on 89–90.
[59] "Theological Implications of Radical Discipleship," in Douglas, *Let the Earth Hear His Voice*, 1294–96.

self-perception, this group was later called "radical evangelicals." Today it represents one of three prominent tendencies in the evangelical movement alongside the traditional evangelicals and the charismatics.[60]

The alternative declaration takes up the positions of the Latin American evangelicals confronting liberation theology. It is based on a concept of man as a total being and of salvation comprising the personal, social, and global dimensions, or involving full-fledged *shalom*. The alternative declaration sees no separation between evangelism and social action, between proclamation of the gospel and its demonstration in the life of God's people: "There is no biblical dichotomy between the Word spoken and the Word made visible in the lives of God's people. Men will look as they listen and what they see must be at one with what they hear" (p. 1294).

For this group, the gospel is the good news of liberation, restoration, fullness, and salvation. The kingdom of God in Jesus Christ is a kingdom of *shalom* that includes a restoration of the whole universe. In the alternative declaration, the theme of the kingdom and the mission of God (*missio Dei*) occupy an important place:

> *We affirm* that the *evangel* is God's Good News in Jesus Christ; it is Good News of the reign he proclaimed and embodies; of God's mission of love to restore the world to wholeness through the Cross of Christ and him alone; of his victory over the demonic posers of destruction and death; of his Lordship over the entire universe. (p. 1294)

> *Strategy for world evangelization* in our generation is with God, from whom we eagerly anticipate the renewal of his community, equipping us with love and power so that the whole Christian community may make known the whole Gospel to the whole man throughout the whole world. (p. 1295)

> *We confess that ...* we have often separated Jesus Christ the Saviour from Jesus Christ the Lord. We have sometimes distorted the biblical understanding of man as a total being and have courted an unbiblical dualism. We have insulated new Christians from life in the world and given simplistic responses to complex problems. ... We have allowed eagerness for qualitative growth to render us silent about the whole counsel of God. (p. 1295-96)

---

[60] For these events, cf. David C. Kirkpatrick, "The Widening of Christian Mission: C. René Padilla and the Intellectual Origins of Integral Mission," in The End of Theology. Shaping Theology for the Sake of Mission, ed. Jason S. Sexton and Paul Weston (Minneapolis: Fortress, 2016), 193-210; Paul Ericksen, "Interview with René Padilla, Billy Graham Center," https://www2.wheaton.edu/bgc/archives/transcripts/cn361t03.pdf. Timothy Chester gives another version of the events in *Awakening to a World of Need: The Recovery of Evangelical Social Concern* (Leicester: IVP, 1993), 82.

Here a holistic and communitarian perspective is present, without the nuances and distinctions that characterize the declarations formulated by Western theologians. There is no priority of evangelism. The relationship between evangelism and social responsibility is not specified; the strategy for world evangelism is a single whole. We can also discern the ripples of the debate around the evangelical response to liberation theology as well as a somewhat anti-Western sentiment, or perhaps a mild resentment toward those who imposed the formulation of the Lausanne Covenant from a completely different perspective.[61]

## Madras and Lima (1979), Pattaya (1980): Social Responsibility

As Lausanne I did not specify the relationship between evangelism and social responsibility, the theologians of the Global South organized regional consultations at which they formulated declarations on the subject. Two of these occurred in 1979: one organized by the All India Conference on Evangelical Social Action in Madras, which composed the Madras Declaration, and the second Latin American Congress on Evangelism (CLADE II) in Peru, which adopted the Lima Letter.

In contrast, a consultation at Pattaya, Thailand in 1980, organized by North American theologians, presents a counterpoint. It was entitled "How Shall They Hear?" and was dominated by the ideas of the church growth movement. The theme of social responsibility was practically absent. The Pattaya Declaration affirms, "We endorse the Lausanne Covenant in its entirety. It remains the basis of our common activity, and nothing it contains is beyond our concern, so long as it is clearly related to world evangelization."[62] Padilla wrote later:

> Quite clearly, the Pattaya Consultation on World Evangelization failed to cope with the debatable issue of the relationship between evangelism and social responsibility. The tension already present in the Lausanne Covenant between ... evangelism and socio-political involvement ... and that "in the church's mission of sacrificial service evangelism is primary" (paragraph 6) remained unresolved.[63]

---

[61] For reflections of this ambience, cf. Valdir R. Steuernagel, "Social Concern and Evangelization: The Journey of the Lausanne Movement," *Occasional Bulletin from the Missionary Research Library* 15, no. 2 (1991): 53–56.

[62] Lausanne Movement, "The Thailand Statement," https://www.lausanne.org/content/statement/thailand-statement.

[63] Padilla, "From Lausanne I to Lausanne III," 9, quoted by Kirkpatrick, *A Gospel for the Poor*, 158.

Theologians of the Global South such as Orlando Costas (Puerto Rico), Vinay Samuel (India), and David Gitari (Kenya), together with Ronald Sider (USA) and Andrew Kirk (UK), formulated a "Declaration of Preoccupations Concerning the Future of the Lausanne Committee for World Evangelization." The document requested that the Lausanne Movement pay more attention to the analysis of social and political realities, concentrate on the relationship between evangelism and social responsibility, and organize a congress within three years. Even though the Lausanne Committee initially rejected this proposal, the Theological Commission of the Lausanne Movement organized two consultations on social questions: one on a simple lifestyle in 1980, and one on evangelism and social responsibility in 1982.[64]

## Hoddesdon, London (1980): A Simple Lifestyle

In 1980, an international consultation under the direction of John Stott and Ron Sider gathered at Hoddesdon in the north part of London. Its "purpose was to study simple living in relation to evangelism, relief and justice, since all three are mentioned in the Lausanne Covenant's sentences on simple life-style."[65] Paragraph 9 of the Lausanne Covenant notes, "Those of us who live in affluent circumstances accept our duty to develop a simple life-style in order to contribute more generously to both relief and evangelism." Paragraph 4 of the "Evangelical Commitment to Simple Lifestyle" established a biblical foundation:

> We rejoice that the church is the new community of the new age, whose members enjoy a new life and a new life-style. The earliest Christian church, constituted in Jerusalem on the Day of Pentecost, was characterized by a quality of fellowship unknown before. Those Spirit-filled believers loved one another to such an extent that they sold and shared their possessions. Although their selling and giving were voluntary, and some private property was retained (Acts 5:4), it was made subservient to the needs of the community. "None of them said that anything he had was his own" (Acts 4:32). That is, they were free from the selfish assertion of proprietary rights. And as a result of their transformed economic relationships, "there was not a needy person among them" (Acts 4:34). This principle of generous and sacrificial sharing, expressed in holding ourselves and our goods available for people in need, is an indispensable characteristic of every Spirit-filled church.

---

[64] René Padilla and Chris Sugden (eds.), *Texts on Evangelical Social Ethics 1974-1983* (Nottingham, UK: Grove, 1985), 11-17, 22-25; Tizon, "Precursors and Tensions in Holistic Mission," 67.

[65] "Lausanne Occasional Paper 20: An Evangelical Commitment to Simple Life-style," https://www.lausanne.org/content/lop/lop-20.

Paragraph 5 moves on to a commitment:

> We intend to re-examine our income and expenditure, in order to manage on less and give away more. We lay down no rules or regulations, for either ourselves or others. Yet we resolve to renounce waste and oppose extravagance in personal living, clothing and housing, travel and church buildings.

This consultation recognized fully the nonverbal aspect of the Christian testimony as an integral part of "our Christian duty," or our social responsibility.

## Grand Rapids (1982): Evangelism and Social Responsibility

After Lausanne I, the debate over the relationship between evangelism and social responsibility continued. While for some the resolutions of Lausanne did not go far enough in recognizing the importance of sociopolitical action, for others they went too far. To specify the position of the Lausanne movement on this matter and to gather the advocates of the two positions around a table, John Stott organized a consultation at Grand Rapids (USA) in 1982 under the patronage of the Lausanne Movement and the World Evangelical Alliance. Stott also formulated the resulting document.[66]

In his preface, Stott presented the context of the consultation. The history of the ecumenical movement in relation to its social commitments had provoked evangelical suspicion. The polarization became very visible in 1980, two years before the consultation, when two parallel conferences took place: on the ecumenical side, "Your Kingdom Come" in Melbourne, and on the evangelical side, "How Shall They Hear?" in Pattaya, Thailand. At Melbourne, the cries of the poor, the hungry and the oppressed predominated; at Pattaya, those of the non-evangelized.

The objectives of the Grand Rapids event were as follows: according to Stott's preface:

> To study Scripture, history, theology and the contemporary church, and the interaction among them, that we shall come to understand each other better and to appreciate each other's points of view more fully; that we shall reach a greater unity of mind on the relationship between evangelism and social

---

[66] "The Grand Rapids Report on Evangelism and Social Responsibility: An Evangelical Commitment," in John Stott, *Making Christ Known: Historic Mission Documents from the Lausanne Movement 1974-1989* (Grand Rapids: Eerdmans, 1996), 185ff; "Lausanne Occasional Paper 21: Evangelism and Social Responsibility: An Evangelical Commitment," https://www.lausanne.org/content/lop/lop-21.

responsibility; ... that we shall commit ourselves, and encourage other believers to commit themselves, to a yet more active fulfilment of our evangelistic and social responsibilities.

Stott further stated, "I confess that I arrived in Grand Rapids with a considerable degree of apprehension." Valdir Steuernagel describes the consultation as the most thoroughly planned, and also the most sensitive, feared, and menacing, ever held by the Lausanne Committee for World Evangelization.[67]

First, the Grand Rapids report took up the definitions of evangelism and social responsibility from the Lausanne Covenant in paragraphs 2 and 3. In paragraph 4, the consultation proposed three models to specify the relationship between evangelism and social responsibility: social action as a *consequence* of evangelism ("one is saved to serve"); social action as a *bridge* toward evangelism; and social action as *partner* of evangelism. Social action and evangelism "are like two blades of scissors or two wings of a bird" (§ 4c).

At Grand Rapids, an important nuance concerning the role of evangelism was also introduced: the document did not speak of "priority" anymore, but of the "primacy" of evangelism (§ 4d). On this question, in the same paragraph 4 it made two propositions. First, social action presupposes converted Christians who are socially responsible. Second, evangelism relates to the eternal destiny of man and is a specific task for Christians. Under these two aspects, one has to recognize a "logical" priority, but not a chronological priority of evangelism.

## Wheaton (1983): The Church in Response to Human Need

In 1983, another consultation took place at Wheaton, following the logic of the alternative declaration of Lausanne. The acts of the consultation, published by the Indian theologian Vinay Samuel together with his British colleague Chris Sugden, take up the perspective of the theologians of the Global South.[68] Paragraph 11 defines transformation, which is one key element marking the importance of this statement:

---

[67] Valdir R. Steuernagel, "The Theology of Mission in Its Relation to Social Responsibility within the Lausanne Movement," Ph.D. thesis, Lutheran School of Theology, Chicago, 1988, 151–56.

[68] Vinay Samuel and Chris Sugden (eds.), *The Church in Response to Human Need* (Grand Rapids: Eerdmans, 1987). For the Consultation Statement, see also *Transformation* 1, no. 1 (1984): 23–28; https://www.lausanne.org/content/statement/transformation-the-church-in-response-to-human-need.

According to the biblical view of human life, then, transformation is the change from a condition of human existence contrary to God's purpose to one in which people are able to enjoy fullness of life in harmony with God (John 10:10; Col. 3:8–15; Eph. 4:13). This transformation can only take place through the obedience of individuals and communities to the Gospel of Jesus Christ, whose power changes the lives of men and women by releasing them from the guilt, power, and consequences of sin, enabling them to respond with love toward God and toward others (Rom. 5:5), and making them "new creatures in Christ" (2 Cor. 5:17) (§ 11).

Paragraph 13 specifies that the goal of transformation is best described by the biblical vision of the reign of God. In paragraph 53, the Statement affirms "that transformation is, in the final analysis, His work, but work in which He engages us. To this end He has given us His Spirit, the Transformer *par excellence*." In 1999, Vinay Samuel proposed a simplified definition of transformation: "Transformation is to enable God's vision of society to be actualized in all relationships, social, economic and spiritual, so that God's will be reflected in human society and his love be experienced by all communities, especially the poor."[69] (From 1983 on, the term "transformation" often replaced the expression "holistic mission" and so it can be understood as a synonym.)

Evaluating this meeting in 1996, David Bosch wrote that "for the first time in an official statement emanating from an international evangelical conference the perennial dichotomy [between evangelism and social responsibility] was overcome."[70]

## Manila (1989): The Whole Gospel to the Whole World

The congress known as Lausanne II gathered people from about 170 countries at Manila. The Manila Manifesto, again formulated under the presidency of John Stott, prolongs the Lausanne Covenant but also nuances it slightly. The historical context of opposition to the ecumenical movement is clearly visible. The two slogans of the congress were "Proclaim Christ until he comes" and "Calling the whole Church to take the whole gospel to the whole world." The Manifesto contains 21 affirmations, followed by 12 paragraphs that develop the theme of the second slogan.

---

[69] Vinay Samuel quoted by Chris Sugden, "Transformational Development: Current State of Understanding and Practice," *Transformation* 20, no. 2 (2003): 71.

[70] Bosch quoted by John Stott, ed., *Making Christ Known: Historic Mission Documents from the Lausanne Movement 1974-1989* (Carlisle, Cumbria, UK: Paternoster Press, 1996), 407.

Affirmation 15 discusses the integrity of Christian witness: "We affirm that we who proclaim the gospel must exemplify it in a life of holiness and love; otherwise our testimony loses its credibility." With a side glance at the socio-political programs of the ecumenical movement, paragraph 1 underscores that "neither human religion, nor human righteousness, nor socio-political programs can save people. Self-salvation of every kind is impossible. Left to themselves, human beings are lost forever." Paragraph 4, entitled "Evangelism and Social Responsibility," affirms the necessity of both actions in a transformed Christian life but still insists on the priority of evangelism, despite the nuances introduced at Grand Rapids:

> The authentic gospel must become visible in the transformed lives ... Evangelism is primary because our chief concern is with the gospel, that all people may have the opportunity to accept Jesus Christ as Lord and Saviour. Yet Jesus not only proclaimed the kingdom of God, he also demonstrated its arrival by works of mercy and power. We are called today to a similar integration of words and deeds. In a spirit of humility we are to preach and teach, minister to the sick, feed the hungry, care for prisoners, help the disadvantaged and handicapped, and deliver the oppressed. While we acknowledge the diversity of spiritual gifts, callings, and contexts, we also affirm that good news and good works are inseparable. ... Our continuing commitment to social action is not a confusion of the kingdom of God with a Christianized society. It is, rather, a recognition that the biblical gospel has inescapable social implications.

Following the input of Grand Rapids, the text emphasizes the diversity of gifts, vocations. and situations in the relationship between evangelism and social responsibility. Paragraphs 5 and 6, entitled "God the Evangelist" and "The Human Witness," respectively, mention the notions of God's mission and spiritual warfare.

One element is not visible in the final document: the predominance of strategic reflection during the congress. The end of the twentieth century saw the prominence of the church growth movement, inspired and developed by Donald McGavran of the Fuller School of World Missions, which analyzes the quantitative growth of churches based on statistics and tools from the social sciences. This was also the time of the "AD 2000 and Beyond" Movement[71] under the direction of Luis Bush, which aspired to "finish the task" of world evangelism before the year 2000 and introduced such concepts as "unreached peoples" and the "10/40 Window."[72]

---

[71] Cf. Manila Manifesto, § 11: "The Challenge of AD 2000 and Beyond."
[72] The 10/40 Window refers to regions of Asia, Africa, and Europe between 10 and 40 degrees north of latitude, regions where two-thirds of the world population live

The theologians from the Global South wanted to go deeper in theological reflection, but felt pushed aside and frustrated; Escobar spoke of a "dialogue of the deaf."[73] He saw at Manila three tendencies in the Lausanne Movement: the American "managerial missiology," the European "postcolonial missiology" (critical of the missionary past linked to colonialism, but still in the Western perspective), and the "critical missiology" of the radical evangelical theologians of the Global South.[74] This typology is similar to that of Henning Wrogemann, who distinguished the neo-evangelical group with its main representatives Billy Graham and John Stott, the "confessing evangelicals" typified by German theologian Peter Beyerhaus, and the radical evangelicals led by Escobar and René Padilla.[75]

Reviewing the first two Lausanne congresses, the preparatory congresses, and the consultations, we see that two personalities greatly influenced the beginnings of the Lausanne Movement and the gathering of the evangelical movement in the second half of the twentieth century: Billy Graham (1918–2018) and John Stott (1921–2011). The two were very close friends and an extraordinary tandem. Graham "had expressed the wish that God use their friendship like that of Wesley and Whitefield."[76] Graham was not only the visionary among the evangelicals gathered at these events, but also a leading promoter by his charisma, his broad acceptance within the evangelical world, and the financial means of his association. According to David Kirkpatrick and Henri Blocher, Stott contributed more than anyone else other than Graham to the growth of the evangelical movement and to the emergence of the Lausanne Movement. Stott was the principal editor of the Lausanne Covenant and the preeminent theologian

---

and where the great religious blocs of Islam, Hinduism, and Buddhism are situated. Many of these areas are deeply affected by poverty and contain numerous people groups unreached by Christianity. This part of the planet, it was argued, would thus deserve priority in missionary efforts. The concept is largely obsolete today because it is based on data from the 1980s and 1990s and because it excludes largely Muslim Indonesia and de-Christianized Europe.

[73] Samuel Escobar, "Lausana II y el peregrinaje de la misiología evangélica," *Boletín Teológico* 36 (1989), quoted by Kirkpatrick, *A Gospel for the Poor*, 156. Cf. also Samuel Escobar, "A Movement Divided: Three Approaches to World Evangelization Stand in Tension with One Another," *Transformation* 8 (October 1991): 7–13; John Stott, "Twenty Years after Lausanne: Some Personal Reflections," *International Bulletin of Missionary Research* 19, no. 1 (1995): 50–55.

[74] Escobar, "A Movement Divided," 12f.

[75] Wrogemann, *Intercultural Theology*, vol. 2: *Theologies of Mission*, 124.

[76] Henri Blocher, "John Stott, Mr Evangelical," *Perspectives missionnaires* 62 (2011): 37.

at the subsequent consultations.[77] Escobar would certainly have placed him in the European group in his typology. Robert Hunt confirmed this evaluation when he concluded that Stott was "linked neither to the pragmatism (and defensiveness) of the American leadership nor to the apparent social radicalism of the Latin American and African theologians."[78] Also, because of Stott's extensive travels with the International Fellowship of Evangelical Students (IFES), including trips to Latin America, he could play the important role of mediator between the different positions of evangelicals during the first meetings.

## Oxford (2001): The Micah Network and Integral Mission

Founded in 1999, the Micah Network is a global Christian community of humanitarian and development organizations and individuals engaged in holistic mission. At its conference in Oxford (UK) in September 2001, several days after the terrorist attacks of September 11, it formulated its basic vision in the "Micah Declaration on Integral Mission."[79] The first objective of the Micah Network is "to motivate and equip a global community of Christians to embrace and practice integral mission." By taking up the term "integral mission" from the Latin American Theological Fraternity, described alternatively by the notion of "transformation" by the International Fellowship for Mission as Transformation (INFEMIT), the Micah Network situated itself within the perspective of the radical evangelicals. René Padilla played an important role in INFEMIT and Micah. The most important contribution of this declaration is the definition of "integral mission":

> Integral mission or holistic transformation is the proclamation and demonstration of the gospel. It is not simply that evangelism and social involvement are to be done alongside each other. Rather, in integral mission our proclamation has social consequences as we call people to love and repentance in all areas of life. And our social involvement has evangelistic consequences as we bear witness to the transforming grace of Jesus Christ. If we ignore the world, we betray the word of God which sends us out to serve the

---

[77] David Kirkpatrick stated, "John Stott's influence upon postwar global evangelicalism was probably unrivaled." Kirkpatrick, *A Gospel for the Poor*, 144; cf. Blocher, "John Stott, Mr Evangelical," 38.

[78] Robert A. Hunt, "The History of the Lausanne Movement," *International Bulletin of Missionary Research* 35, no. 2 (2011): 83.

[79] "Micah Declaration on Integral Mission," https://www.micahnetwork.org/?s=micah+declaration+on+integral+mission.

world. If we ignore the word of God, we have nothing to bring to the world. Justice and justification by faith, worship and political action, the spiritual and the material, personal change and structural change, belong together. As in the life of Jesus, being, doing and saying are at the heart of the integral task.

The great value of the notion of integral mission is to unite what Western theology separated previously: evangelism and social responsibility, the spiritual and material domains. "As in the life of Jesus, being, doing and saying are at the heart of the integral task." How can we think practically about this integration? The proposition expressed at Grand Rapids regarding the relationship between social action and evangelism was that social action can be the bridge to, the consequence or the partner of evangelism. Does this really specify the proper way of conceiving the integration? I believe it is clear that the integration of being, saying, and doing in all aspects of life is certainly one of the great challenges for the Church today.

However, the danger inherent in the concept of "integral mission" is the suppression of all distinctions and nuances. Recall that Grand Rapids proposed the nuance of the "primacy" of evangelism rather than "priority" as formulated in the Lausanne Covenant and the Manila Manifesto. The Manifesto equally presented some distinctions by mentioning the diversity of gifts, vocations, and situations.

## Pattaya (2004): Holistic Mission

At the Lausanne Forum for World Evangelization at Pattaya, Thailand, in 2004, one of the thirty-one issue groups treated the subject of holistic mission and produced Lausanne Occasional Paper number 33. René Padilla presented the main paper. The work of the issue group was divided into four sectors: economy, health, hunger/agriculture/water, and relief. A specialist in each sector was commissioned to prepare a paper. Bryant Myers presented on "Humanitarian Response to Uprooted People." In the introduction to Lausanne Occasional Paper 33, Dewi Hughes defined holistic mission as follows: "Holistic mission is the task of bringing the whole of life under the lordship of Jesus Christ. ... The mission of the church is, therefore, comprehensive in its means and in its impact. In this broad sense every Issue Group at the Forum should have been concerned with holistic mission" (3).

The paper presented by René Padilla was endorsed by the Holistic Mission Issue Group not only as their biblical foundation but for Christian mission as a whole (3). After discussing the historical development of the conception of mission, Padilla mentioned Rodger Bassham's evaluation of the impact of the Lausanne Congress: "[It] produced some marked changes in evangelical mission theology ... through broadening the focus ... from evangelism to mission" (6).[80] This affirmation, as we have seen, presupposes a narrow definition of evangelism and a broad conception of mission.

Speaking about the biblical basis of holistic mission (10), Padilla sees three possible approaches to a proper integration of the various constituent elements of the church's mission. These three approaches differ, according to Padilla, only in their focus and are really different parts of one picture.

The first approach takes as its starting point the purpose of God, which embraces the whole of creation. In this perspective,

> Mission is faithful to Scripture only to the extent to which it is holistic. In other words, it is faithful when it crosses frontiers (not just geographic but also cultural, racial, economic, social, political, etc.) with the intention of transforming human life in all its dimensions. ... The reduction of the Christian mission to the oral communication of a message of otherworldly salvation grows out of a misunderstanding of God's purpose. (11)

The second approach takes into account that the human being is a unity of body, soul, and spirit (11). "From this perspective, holistic mission is mission oriented towards the satisfaction of basic human needs, including the need of God, but also the need of food, love, housing, clothes, physical and mental health and a sense of human dignity" (12).

The third approach takes as its starting point the Christ-event, "including Christ's life and ministry, his death on the cross, his resurrection and his exaltation" (12). Padilla then develops the holistic dimensions of each element of the Christ-event (12–17). In an historical perspective on holistic mission, he emphasizes the socioeconomic impact of the Moravian, Pietistic, and revivalist missions along with their accent on the eternal destiny of men. With regard to the role of the local church and of Christian NGOs, Padilla notes an important deficiency of evangelical theology, in ecclesiology. Quoting the Micah Declaration on Integral Mission (2001), he calls for "caring and inclusive communities":

> God by his grace has given local churches the task of integral mission [proclaiming and demonstrating the gospel]. The future of integral mission is in

---

[80] Rodger C. Bassham, *Mission Theology: 1948-1975, Years of Worldwide Creative Tension: Ecumenical, Evangelical, and Roman Catholic* (Pasadena, CA: William Carey Library, 1979), 231, quoted by Padilla, "Holistic Mission," in Lausanne Occasional Paper no. 31, 6.

planting and enabling local churches to transform the communities of which they are part. Churches as caring and inclusive communities are at the heart of what it means to do integral mission. (19)

In summary, the Holistic Mission Issue Group at the Lausanne Forum at Pattaya reasoned in line with the alternative declaration from Lausanne and the Micah Declaration on Integral Mission, both inspired by René Padilla.

## Cape Town (2010): Love God and Serve the World

The third congress for world evangelization in Cape Town (Lausanne III) gathered 4,200 evangelical leaders from 198 countries and reached out to hundreds of thousands more participants by transmission over the internet. The Lausanne Movement and the World Evangelical Alliance were the conference sponsors. Padilla endorsed the claim by Doug Birdsall, Lausanne's executive president, that Cape Town was the "the most globally representative assembly of evangelicals in history." [81]This congress fully exhibited what Andrew Walls called Christianity's "transfer of the centre of gravity" toward the South and East, in that the great majority of the participants came from the "majority world." The general theme of the congress was that "God was in Christ, reconciling the world to himself" (2 Cor 5:19). The specific themes for every day represented "the greatest challenges for the Church during the ten years to come": truth, reconciliation, priorities, integrity, and partnerships.

Stott was no longer presiding over the formulation of the Cape Town Commitment,[82] succeeded by a group of mainly majority-world theologians under the direction of Christopher Wright. On one hand, we can see historical continuity with the Lausanne Covenant and the Manila Manifesto. The Cape Town Commitment extends these statements, updates them, and applies them to the 21st-century context. In this vein, it introduces such themes as diaspora, oral cultures, megacities, the prosperity gospel, spiritual warfare, drugs, and human trafficking. On the other hand, the Cape Town Commitment introduces several new elements. First, it is eight times longer than the Lausanne Covenant and three times longer than the Manila Manifesto. The terminology changes from "evangelism" in the first two documents to "reconciliation" and

---

[81] C. René Padilla, "The Future of the Lausanne Movement," *International Bulletin of Missionary Research* 35, no. 2 (2011): 86.

[82] Lausanne Movement, "The Cape Town Commitment: A Confession of Faith and a Call to Action," https://www.lausanne.org/content/ctcommitment#capetown.

"witness," from "mission" and "missionary" to "integral mission" and "missional." Thematically, it is centered entirely on love. Although many Christians know and cherish John 3:16, the theme of love was relatively marginal in evangelical missiology until the Cape Town Commitment. The language of love gives a relational character to this document. Furthermore, it adopts in great part the holistic perspective encountered in the alternative declaration of Lausanne and the Micah Declaration on Integral Mission. Finally, the Commitment does not contain theological affirmations like the former declarations, but is composed of a "confession of faith" and a "call to action" formulated in a language very close to ecumenical terminology. In fact, there are certain convergences between the "Edinburgh 2010 Common Call," the document of an ecumenical meeting, and the Cape Town Commitment. Not only does the Commitment adopt a relational and holistic perspective, found usually among the theologians of the Global South, but it also calls for the practical application of the gospel, an element emphasized by the Latin American theologians faced with liberation theology and its notion of praxis and by the theologians of INFEMIT who favor the terminology of transformation.

Concerning the relationship between evangelism and social responsibility, the Commitment pursues more a logic of "integration" than of distinctions. In this vein, it picks up the definitions of evangelism by the Lausanne Covenant and of integral mission by the Micah Network in paragraph 10b of its first part. This perspective of integration is also part of the relational worldviews. Rather than pairing "evangelism and social responsibility" based on a dichotomizing worldview, the Cape Town Commitment speaks of "evangelism and transformation" (II.A, 3), an important nuance within the framework of a holistic worldview. These observations could be explained by the fact that most of the theologians in the group editing the Commitment came from the Global South and thus from continents with typically relational and holistic worldviews. The president of the editing group, Christopher Wright, an Old Testament specialist, spent many years in missionary service in India, a subcontinent characterized generally by a relational and holistic worldview. Wright's book *The Mission of God* defends a holistic conception of mission.[83] He uses the adjective "missional" in his book and in the Commitment with the same broad meaning. Wright's broad concept of mission surfaces, for example, in the following passage of the Commitment:

---

[83] Christopher J. H. Wright, *The Mission of God: Unlocking God's Narrative* (Downers Grove: IVP, 2006).

> Our engagement in mission ... in all its dimensions: evangelism, bearing witness to the truth, discipling, peace-making, social engagement, ethical transformation, caring for creation, overcoming evil powers, casting out demonic spirits, healing the sick, suffering and enduring under persecution. (I, 5C)

Probably because of these changes in the direction of a holistic worldview and the practical implications of witness, René Padilla evaluated the Cape Town Commitment positively:

> I am happy about the content of the Cape Town Commitment. ... It is a remarkable document. For my part, I have looked for three things: (1) globalization and poverty; (2) a call to radical discipleship; and (3) a preoccupation with ecology. I have found all these points, and I am very happy how they were treated.[84]

But Padilla criticized the Lausanne Movement for its preoccupation with evangelism strategies (according to him a primarily U.S. approach),[85] the dichotomy between evangelical spirituality and social responsibility, the insufficient space given to theological reflection, and a lack of consideration of contextual factors and of the shift of Christianity's center of gravity to the south and east. He objected that "the locus of organizational leadership, control of financial resources and strategic decision-making tends to remain with the north and the west."[86]

## Bangkok (2011): Christian Witness in a Multi-religious World

The Pontifical Council for Interreligious Dialogue (PCID), the World Council of Churches (WCC), and, at the WCC's invitation, the World Evangelical Alliance (WEA) met during a period of five years to reflect and produce a document entitled "Christian Witness in a Multi-religious World."[87] The participants in the third consultation of this series met in Bangkok, Thailand, in 2011 and finalized the document. Even though it was not intended

---

[84] Conversation between René Padilla and Doug Birdsall on August 3, 2012, according to Doug Birdsall's email to Lausanne leaders, quoted by Jean-Paul Rempp, "Le Mouvement de Lausanne après le Cap: Évolution et perspectives," *Théologie évangélique* 11, no. 3 (2012): 143 (my translation).
[85] Wilbert Shenk claims with Padilla and Escobar that in the Lausanne Movement, strategic reflections predominate over theological reflections. Wilbert R. Shenk, "2004 Forum for World Evangelization: A Report," *International Bulletin of Missionary Research* 29, no. 2 (2005): 31; cf. Escobar, "A Movement Divided."
[86] Padilla, "The Future of the Lausanne Movement," 87.
[87] The document can be found at https://www.worldevangelicals.org/pdf/1106 Christian_Witness_in_a_Multi-Religio us_World.pdf.

to be a theological statement on mission, it recommends some principles for Christian witness and conduct:

> 1. *Acting in God's love.* Christians believe that God is the source of all love and, accordingly, in their witness they are called to live lives of love and to love their neighbour as themselves (cf. Matthew 22:34–40; John 14:15).
>
> 2. *Imitating Jesus Christ.* In all aspects of life, and especially in their witness, Christians are called to follow the example and teachings of Jesus Christ, sharing his love, giving glory and honour to God the Father in the power of the Holy Spirit (cf. John 20:21–23).
>
> 3. *Christian virtues.* Christians are called to conduct themselves with integrity, charity, compassion and humility, and to overcome all arrogance, condescension and disparagement (cf. Galatians 5:22).
>
> 4. *Acts of service and justice.* Christians are called to act justly and to love tenderly (cf. Micah 6:8). They are further called to serve others and in so doing to recognize Christ in the least of their sisters and brothers (cf. Matthew 25:45). Acts of service, such as providing education, health care, relief services and acts of justice and advocacy are an integral part of witnessing to the gospel. ...
>
> 5. *Discernment in ministries of healing.* As an integral part of their witness to the gospel, Christians exercise ministries of healing.

In summary, the document of this inter-Christian consultation adopts a broad view of mission in line with the developments in the Roman Catholic Church and the ecumenical and evangelical movements at the end of the twentieth and the beginning of the twenty-first centuries.

## Conclusion

Our historical overview of the evangelical declarations has brought to light three tensions related to the concept of mission. There are missiological debates first over the scope of the semantic domain of mission, and second around the relationship between evangelism and social responsibility in missions. Third, there is also a conflict between theologies of the Global North and South in relation to Christianity's transfer of the center of gravity.[88] Having observed a considerable development of the first two

---

[88] Cf. J. Kevin Livingston, "A Missiology of the Road: The Theology of Mission and Evangelism of David J. Bosch," Ph.D. thesis, University of Aberdeen, 1989, 107–89; Tizon, "Precursors and Tensions in Holistic Mission," 72–74.

tensions, I would suggest that the worldview of the theologians influences Bible interpretation and the conception of theologies, in this case theologies of mission. Summing up the debate in a more generalizing and schematic way, the dichotomizing concept of mission has developed into a holistic concept simultaneously with Christianity's shift toward the south. This dependence of Bible interpretation and of theological conceptions on worldviews evidently relativizes certain theological positions. In the next chapter, we will consider how this contingency can be contained.

From the historical point of view, such an enlargement of the semantic domain of mission also occurred in the ecumenical movement during the second half of the twentieth century, some decades before the similar development in the evangelical movement. One consequence was that the interest in missions has diminished markedly within the ecumenical movement since then. As David Hesselgrave remarks, "The missionary endeavor was marginalized in part because the ecumenical vision of mission was gradually broadened by the WCC to include everything the church does in the world—and even what God does outside the church."[89]

Charles van Engen provides more detail, attributing this loss of mission motivation to three factors: the integration of the International Missionary Council into the World Council of Churches, the incorporation of the concept of *missio Dei* as the foundation of the theology of mission, and the affirmation that the Church is missionary by its nature.[90] Another consequence, a logical result of the first one, is that the number of missionaries sent out by the Protestant mainline denominations has dwindled to only a very small percentage of the total number of missionaries.[91] What will be the result of this same development in the evangelical movement?

## Further Reading

The declarations of the Lausanne Movement can be found on its web site: https://www.lausanne.org.

Černý, Pavel, "John Stott (1921–2011), Radical Disciple of Christ: On the Centenary of His Birth and the Tenth Anniversary of His Death," *European Journal of Theology* 30, no. 1 (2021): 7–17.

---

[89] Hesselgrave, *Paradigms in Conflict*, 323.
[90] Charles van Engen, *Mission on the Way. Issues in Mission Theology* (Grand Rapids: Baker, 1996), 157.
[91] Paul E. Pierson, "Lessons from the Twentieth Century: Conciliar Missions," in *Between Past and Future: Evangelical Mission Entering the Twenty-first Century*, ed. Jonathan Bonk (Pasadena: William Carey Library, 2003), 67–84, quoted by Hesselgrave, *Paradigms in Conflict*, 317.

Engelsviken, Tormod, "Mission, Evangelism and Evangelization: From the Perspective of the Lausanne Movement," *International Review of Mission* 96 (2007): 204–9.

Escobar, Samuel, "A Movement Divided: Three Approaches to World Evangelization Stand in Tension with One Another," *Transformation* 8, no. 4 (1991): 7–13.

Glasser, Arthur F., "The Evolution of Evangelical Mission Theology since World War II," *International Bulletin of Missionary Research* 6 (1985): 9–13.

Padilla, C. René, "The Future of the Lausanne Movement," *International Bulletin of Missionary Research* 35, no. 2 (2011): 86–88.

Schreiter, Robert J., "From the Lausanne Covenant to the Cape Town Commitment. A Theological Assessment," *International Bulletin of Missionary Research* 35, no. 2 (2011): 88–92.

Stott, John, *Christian Mission in the Modern World* (Downers Grove: IVP, 2013; 1st ed. London: Falcon, 1975).

Stott, John, "Twenty Years after Lausanne: Some Personal Reflections," *International Bulletin of Missionary Research* 19, no. 1 (1995): 50–55.

Sugden, Christopher, "Theological Developments since Lausanne I," *Transformation* 7, no. 1 (1990): 9–12.

# Chapter 2

## Holistic Mission and the Definition of Mission: A Biblical and Theological Perspective

In this chapter, I evaluate the missiological debate over the definition of mission, particularly the concept of holistic mission, in the light of worldview perspectives and the Bible. This evaluation is necessary because competing understandings of the concept of mission have become a problem to which no solution is yet visible on the horizon.

### Evangelism and Mission in the Missiological Debate

In this first section, I sum up the development of the missiological debate concerning the definition of mission and the relationship between evangelism and social responsibility. I undertake this review first through a historical analysis and then by comparing two typologies. After that, I present some propositions for a "multiple witness," a holistic concept of mission combining multiple partial approaches to mission.

#### Historical Development of the Missiological Debate

In the first chapter, we had to wade through a large number of definitions of evangelism and mission. The various authors used the terms in diverse ways, and the definitions are not as clear as their frequent use would seem to suggest.

Some authors use evangelism and mission in a fairly synonymous manner, covering the whole spectrum from narrow to broad conceptions. Others distinguish evangelism and mission, for example by assigning the word "evangelism" to local and mono-cultural approaches and "mission" to cross-cultural activities. Another distinction connects evangelism to activities targeted toward those who are nominal Christians or have disassociated themselves from Christianity, and mission to those who are *not yet* Christians. This point of view is common among Lutheran and Reformed thinkers and in Vatican II documents. Among those who distinguish between the two terms, for some evangelism is a broader term covering the whole ministry of the Church outside of its walls, while for others it is a narrower term covering only the verbal proclamation of the gospel. The Catholic Church, for example, has opted for the expression "new evangelism" by assigning to the term a very broad semantic domain. On the other hand, the Lausanne Movement speaks of world evangelization and narrows the term to verbal proclamation of the gospel.[92]

One way to orient oneself in this chaos is through a historical approach to the development of the definitions in the declarations of the Lausanne Movement and their evaluation by theologians and missiologists. The reason why the Lausanne Movement has avoided the term "mission" seems to be the enlargement of the concept in ecumenical and Catholic circles during the period before the first Lausanne congress in 1974. The term "evangelization" seemed to avoid misunderstandings.[93]

According to the definition in paragraph 4 of the Lausanne Covenant, evangelism entails presence, dialogue, proclamation, and persuasion. The missing element here in relation to a holistic definition of mission is social action. This aspect is included in the holistic concept of mission by the Latin American and African authors of the alternative declaration of Lausanne. Paragraph 5 of the Lausanne Covenant then mentions social action, aiming at a balance between a dichotomizing view (evangelism and social responsibility, a "Northern" outlook) and a holistic or "Southern" view, and referring to both as "part of our Christian duty." This formulation reflects John Stott's mediating position. He was responsible for the formulation of the first declarations within our time period of interest, at (1974), Grand Rapids (1982), and Manila (1989). In consequence, in the Grand Rapids statement, evangelism still takes priority over social responsibility. Concerning the relationship between the two, the Grand Rapids Report proposes that social action is either a *consequence* of evangelism, a *bridge* toward evangelism, or its *partner*. For Grand Rapids, there is no dichotomy in the Bible:

> We tend to set over against one another in an unhealthy way soul and body, the individual and society, redemption and creation, grace and nature, heaven and earth, justification and justice, faith and works. The Bible

---

[92] For a detailed discussion, cf. David J. Bosch, "Evangelism: Theological Currents and Cross-Currents Today," *International Bulletin of Missionary Research* 3 (1987): 98–103.

[93] Ralph Winter, "The Highest Priority: Cross-Cultural Evangelism," in *Let the Earth Hear His Voice: Official Reference Volume, Papers and Responses*, International Congress on World Evangelization Lausanne, ed. James D. Douglas (Minneapolis: World Wide Publications, 1975), 213–25; David J. Bosch, *Transforming Mission: Paradigm Shifts in Theology of Mission* (Maryknoll: Orbis, 1996), 411.

certainly distinguishes between these, but also relates them to each other, and it instructs us to hold each pair in a dynamic and creative tension.[94]

In John Stott's words, the two are like the two wings of a bird. The Manila Manifesto (1989) affirms the necessary integration of evangelism and social responsibility:

> We are called today to a similar integration of words and deeds [as in Jesus' ministry]. In a spirit of humility, we are to preach and teach, minister to the sick, feed the hungry, care for prisoners, help the disadvantaged and handicapped, and deliver the oppressed. While we acknowledge the diversity of spiritual gifts, callings, and contexts, we also affirm that good news and good works are inseparable.[95]

Ronald Sider went even further in articulating this integration when reacting in 1979 to the positions of Lausanne I (1974):

> The time has come for all Christians to refuse to use the sentence: "The primary task of the Church is … ." I do not care if you complete the sentence with evangelism or social action. Either way it is unbiblical and misleading. Evangelism, seeking social justice, fellowship, teaching, worship are all fundamental dimensions of the total task of the church. They must not be confused with each other although they are inextricably interrelated.[96]

Sider clearly favored a holistic perspective. On the other hand, David Bosch pursued Stott's perspective in *Transforming Mission* (1991). He distinguished between evangelism and mission, the former being the narrower concept:

> Evangelism [is] that dimension and activity of the church's mission which, by word and deed and in the light of particular conditions and a particular context, offers every person and community, everywhere, a valid opportunity to be directly challenged to a radical reorientation of their lives, a reorientation which involves such things as deliverance from slavery to the world and its powers; embracing Christ as Saviour and Lord; becoming a living member of his community, the church; being enlisted into his service of

---

[94] Lausanne Movement, *Evangelism and Social Responsibility: An Evangelical Commitment*, Lausanne Occasional Paper 21: The Grand Rapids Report, 4A, https://www.lausanne.org/content/lop/lop-21.

[95] "Manilla Manifesto," paragraph 4, https://www.lausanne.org/content/manifesto/the-manila-manifesto.

[96] Ronald J. Sider, "Words and Deeds," *Journal of Theology for Southern Africa* 29 (December 1979): 47.

reconciliation, peace, and justice on earth; and being committed to God's purpose of placing all things under the rule of Christ.[97]

For Bosch, "evangelism is the core, heart, or centre of mission; it consists in the proclamation of salvation in Christ to non-believers."[98] However, in the eighteenth affirmation on evangelism, Bosch specifies, "Evangelism is not only verbal proclamation." His position differs thus from that of most evangelical authors, who opt for a narrow conception of evangelism and perceive it as strictly verbal proclamation of the gospel. On the other hand, for Bosch, "mission denotes the total task God has set the church for the salvation of the world. ... Mission is the church sent into the world, to love, to serve, to preach, to teach, to heal, to liberate."[99] Bosch has thus a broad concept of mission.

In 2007, the Theological Working Group of the Lausanne Movement asked Tormod Engelsviken, one of its members, during one of its consultations at the Bossey Institute in Geneva, to define mission, evangelism, and evangelization so as to express the consensus of the Lausanne Movement on the subject. He defined the terms in a similar way to Bosch:

> Although there is no consistent way of speaking of mission, evangelization and evangelism within the Lausanne movement, we may say that while mission and evangelization are the broader, more comprehensive terms including both proclamation and social concern, evangelism is a more narrow [sic] concept being defined primarily in terms of proclamation.[100]

The difficulty of defining evangelism and mission was not resolved in the Lausanne Movement before the change of the millennium. Meanwhile, in 2001 the Micah Network entered into a new stage by introducing the concept of integral mission, thereby adopting the holistic approach promoted by the theologians of the Global South. The Cape Town Commitment took up this concept in 2010, in a section with the heading "Bearing witness to the truth of Christ in a pluralistic, globalized world":

---

[97] David J. Bosch, *Transforming Mission: Paradigm Shifts in Theology of Mission* (Maryknoll: Orbis, 1996), 420. See also his eighteen affirmations on evangelism, on pages 411–20.
[98] Bosch, "Evangelism: Theological Currents and Cross-Currents Today," 100.
[99] Bosch, *Transforming Mission*, 554.
[100] Tormod Engelsviken, "Mission, Evangelism and Evangelization—from the Perspective of the Lausanne Movement," *International Review of Mission* vol. 96, no. 382/383 (July-October 2007): 205.

> As disciples of Christ we are called to be people of truth. (1) We must *live* the truth. To live the truth is to be the face of Jesus, through whom the glory of the gospel is revealed to blinded minds. People will see truth in the faces of those who live their lives for Jesus, in faithfulness and love. (2) We must *proclaim* the truth. Spoken proclamation of the truth of the gospel remains paramount in our mission. This cannot be separated from living out the truth. Works and words must go together. (II.I.1A)

By choosing and defining the term "witness," the Cape Town Commitment avoids the terms "evangelism" and "mission," both frequently open to misunderstandings. The Commitment starts with a call to *"live* the truth" and continues with *"proclaim* the truth." Nine years earlier, the Micah Network still started with proclamation. The Lausanne Movement, now dominated by the theologians of the Global South with a more holistic worldview, seems to recognize a holistic approach to mission and the importance of non-verbal communication.

However, not all evangelical Western theologians follow this conception. Many prefer a narrow definition of evangelism as verbal proclamation, distinguished from the broader view of mission that incorporates the priority of evangelism. For example, David Hesselgrave, professor emeritus of missiology at Trinity Evangelical Divinity School in Chicago (USA), insists that "the primary concern of our Lord has to do with meeting spiritual needs, not with meeting physical, material, or social needs."[101] To underscore this point, he quotes Luke 19:10: "For the Son of Man came to seek out and to save the lost" (cf. Mk 10:45). Carl Braaten, professor emeritus of systematic theology at the Lutheran School of Theology in Chicago (USA), writes in the same vein, contending that holistic mission "has contributed to such a great inflation in the meaning of mission, including virtually everything the church is doing, that there is a danger that evangelism, which is the heart of mission, will become buried in an avalanche of church activism.[102]

## Typological Syntheses of the Missiological Debate

I turn now from the historical analysis to a typological synthesis. Two missiologists have summed up the debate by typologies: the German Henning Wrogemann and the David Hesselgrave of the United States.

---

[101] David J. Hesselgrave, "Holism and Prioritism: For Whom Is the Gospel Good News?" in *Paradigms in Conflict: 10 Key Questions in Christian Missions Today* (Grand Rapids: Kregel, 2005), 136.

[102] Carl Braaten, *The Apostolic Imperative: Nature and Aim of the Church's Mission and Ministry* (Minneapolis: Augsburg, 1985), 111.

## Typology according to Henning Wrogemann

Henning Wrogemann synthesizes the historical development of the relationship between evangelism and social responsibility by a typology that includes five models, moving from a dichotomizing to a holistic perspective.[103]

He starts with the *diastatic model*, according to which evangelism and social action are separate. Mission is understood as proclamation of the Word with the aim of salvation and church planting and thus becomes a synonym of evangelism. Social action is seen as secondary and distinct from mission. Typical representatives of this view, according to Wrogemann, are the church growth movement initiated by Donald McGavran, the AD2000 and Beyond movement, certain fundamentalist groups in the USA, and certain advocates of a premillennialist eschatology. John Stott at the time of the 1966 Berlin congress also reflected this model.

Second is the *preparatory model*: social action prepares for evangelism and serves it. It is seen as an occasion for "points of contact" and as a "bridge" for evangelism. It sets the foundation for evangelism, *the* thing that counts. This view is well illustrated by the following quotation of Harold Lindsell, one of the main organizers of the 1966 Wheaton congress: "Service is a means to an end. As long as service makes it possible to confront men with the gospel, it is useful."[104] We can perceive here one of the positions proposed at Grand Rapids in 1982. Would social action not run the risk of serving as a bait in this case?

The third option is the *consecutive model*: social action as a consequence of evangelism and as visible demonstration of the gospel. According to Wrogemann, Billy Graham and Arthur P. Johnston, among others, defended this model.[105] For them, social action is the work of persons who are born again in Christ. This model presupposes previously converted Christians who are socially responsible (and thus prior evangelism). We can recognize here another model proposed at Grand Rapids in 1982.

---

[103] Henning Wrogemann, *Intercultural Theology*, vol. 2: *Theologies of Mission*, trans. Karl E. Böhmer (Downers Grove, IL: IVP Academic, 2018), 126–28. Wrogemann draws on Erhard Berneburg's more detailed typology in *Das Verhältnis von Verkündigung und sozialer Aktion in der evangelikalen Missionstheorie* (Wuppertal: Brockhaus, 1997), 106–48.

[104] Harold Lindsell, "A Rejoinder," *International Review of Mission* 54 (October 1965): 439.

[105] Arthur P. Johnston, *The Battle for World Evangelization* (Wheaton: Tyndale, 1978). Johnston wrote this book on behalf of Billy Graham (cf. the preface, p. 12).

Fourth, in the *complementary model*, social action and evangelism are seen as complementary dimensions of mission, or the two wings of a bird. According to the later Stott, "neither is a means to the other, or even a manifestation of the other. For each is an end in itself. Both are expressions of unfeigned love."[106] Both are indispensable for mission. Stott and the Lausanne Movement have progressively adopted this position. The radical evangelicals such as Samuel Escobar, René Padilla, Vinay Samuel, Jim Wallis, Ronald Sider, and Christopher Sugden have adhered to this position since 1973. Sider summarizes it in this way:

> Evangelism and social action are intricately interrelated. They are inseparable both in the sense that evangelism often leads to increased social justice and vice versa and also that biblical Christians will, precisely to the extent that they are faithful followers of Jesus, always seek liberty for the oppressed (Luke 4:18). But the fact that evangelism and social action are inseparable certainly does not mean that they are identical. They are distinct, equally important parts of the total mission of the church.[107]

The radical evangelicals have expressed this position in the Chicago Declaration of Evangelical Social Concern in 1973 and in the Micah Declaration on Integral Mission in 2001.

Fifth and finally, the *identification model* does not distinguish social action and evangelism. The positions of the General Assembly of the World Council of Churches at Uppsala in 1968 and the Commission for World Mission and Evangelism conference at Bangkok in 1973 are close to this model. According to the formulation by Emilio Castro, first Director of the Evangelism and Mission Commission of the WCC and later its General Secretary, "evangelism only exists where there is social concern. Without it there may be propaganda, proselytism, but hardly good news."[108]

---

[106] John Stott, *Christian Mission in the Modern World* (London: Falcon, 1975; Downers Grove: IVP, 2013), 43.

[107] Ronald J. Sider, "Evangelism, Salvation, and Social Justice," in *The Study of Evangelism: Exploring a Missional Practice of the Church*, ed. Paul W. Chilcote and Laceye C. Warner (Grand Rapids: Eerdmans, 2008), 203.

[108] Emilio Castro, "Evangelism and Social Justice," *Ecumenical Review* 20, no. 2 (1968): 148.

Table 2: Typology of Models according to Henning Wrogemann

| Diastatic Model | Preparatory Model | Consecutive Model | Complementary Model | Identification Model |
|---|---|---|---|---|
| Evangelism and mission as synonyms designating the verbal proclamation of the gospel; social action secondary and distinct | Social action prepares for evangelism and serves it; it is a means to points of contact and as a bridge to evangelism | Social action as consequence of evangelism and as visible demonstration of the gospel | Social action and evangelism as indispensable and complementary dimensions of mission | Social action and evangelism without any distinction |
| Berlin (1966) | Wheaton (1966), Grand Rapids (1982) | Billy Graham and Arthur P. Johnston, Grand Rapids (1982) | John Stott, Lausanne Movement, radical evangelicals | WCC at Uppsala (1968) and CWME at Bangkok (1973) |

In summary, whereas the diastatic model concentrates on redemption and loses sight of God's action in creation, the identification model risks canceling the distinction between the two. The preparatory and consecutive models render one element dependent on the other. Only the complementary model, defended according to Wrogemann's evaluation by Stott, the Lausanne Movement, the radical evangelicals and the Micah Network, seems to do justice to both the distinction between and interdependence of the different dimensions of the Church's global task.

*Typology according to David Hesselgrave*

Missiologist David Hesselgrave conceives a typology that covers the spectrum from the liberationist, holistic view to a position that defends the traditional priority of evangelism. He asks the underlying question of for whom the gospel is good news.[109] Here I present Hesselgrave's typology in the opposite order, which corresponds better to the historical develop-

---

[109] Hesselgrave, *Paradigms in Conflict*, 119–22.

ment of the theological options. Table 3 provides a schematic summary of Hesselgrave's typology.[110]

The option that maintains the *traditional priority* of evangelism fully recognizes the value of social ministries in medicine, education, agriculture, and the economy, but speaks of them as "secondary" or "supporting" ministries. Hesselgrave specifies:

> With reference to spiritual transformation and social transformation, it gives priority to spiritual transformation. With reference to spirit, mind, and body, it gives priority to the spirit or soul. With reference to social action and evangelism, it gives priority to evangelism. In maintaining these priorities, however, it does not admit to being reductionistic.[111]

The conclusion of the Berlin Declaration (1966) is a typical example:

> Our Lord Jesus Christ, to whom belongs all authority in heaven and on earth, has not called us only to him, but has sent us into the world in order that we be his witnesses. In the power of the Spirit, he has mandated us to proclaim the Good News of salvation by his death and resurrection to all the peoples; to invite them to discipleship through repentance and faith; to baptize them in the communion of his Church; and to teach them all his words.[112]

According to Hesselgrave, this high priority of evangelism motivated Billy Graham to finance the Berlin congress, *Christianity Today* to organize it, and Arthur Johnston to defend it twelve years later in *The Battle for World Evangelism* (1978).

The second alternative, *holism*, can be represented by a variety of positions according to the meaning attributed to holism. Some perceive the holistic approach as encompassing word, act, and sign; others in the ministry to the whole person, body, soul and spirit; still others in the partnership between evangelism and social action; and finally others in the transformation of the whole world.

The first type of holism, *restrained holism*, tries to preserve the traditional priority of evangelism. Evangelism and social action are here more or less equal partners. As the Lausanne Covenant states in paragraph 6, "In the Church's mission of sacrificial service, evangelism is primary." John Stott, whom Hesselgrave places in this category, avers that the missionary mandate in John 20:21 is most important: "As the Father has sent me, so I send you." Like the mandate in Luke 4:18f, this mandate takes precedence over Matthew

---

[110] Adapted from Hesselgrave, *Paradigms in Conflict*, 122.
[111] Hesselgrave, *Paradigms in Conflict*, 121.
[112] Arthur P. Johnston, *The Battle for World Evangelism* (Wheaton: Tyndale, 1978), 368f.

28:18–20 since a more holistic vision has begun to permeate evangelicals. Luke 4:18 says, "The Spirit of the Lord is upon me, because he has anointed me to bring good news to the poor. He has sent me to proclaim release to the captives and recovery of sight to the blind, to let the oppressed go free."

The second holism option, *revisionist holism*, sees evangelism and social action as equal partners. Bryant Myers, professor of transformational development at Fuller Theological Seminary, rejects "every dichotomy between the material and the spiritual, between evangelism and social action, between the love of God and the love of our neighbour."[113] James Engel and William Dyrness describe this type of holism in their book, *Changing the Mind of Missions* (2000), as follows:

> Partnership affirms that evangelism and social transformation are inseparable elements in Christ's kingdom that embraces all of creation (Lk 4:18-20). The goal is *shalom*, a sense of human welfare and well-being that transcends an artificial distinction between the private and public worlds. Shalom, by its very nature, is rooted in justice and compassion.[114]

*Table 3: Typology of Options according to David Hesselgrave*

| Traditional Priority | Restrained Holism | Revisionist Holism | Radical Liberation |
|---|---|---|---|
| The mission is primarily to make disciples of all nations. Other Christian ministries are secondary and supportive. | The mission is to minister to society and individuals socially and spiritually while giving a certain priority to evangelism. | The mission is to minister to society and individuals without dichotomizing between the physical and spiritual or the body and soul/spirit. | The mission is to promote justice in society and establish *Shalom* on the earth. |
| Billy Graham, Arthur P. Johnston, Berlin (1966) | John Stott, Lausanne Movement | Bryant Myers | Gustavo Gutiérrez, liberation theology |

---

[113] Bryant Myers, *Walking with the Poor: Principles and Practices of Transformational Development* (Monrovia, CA: World Vision, 1999); cf. Myers, "In Response ... Another Look at Holistic Mission," *Evangelical Missions Quarterly* 35, no. 3 (1999): 287; Myers, "Holistic Mission: New Frontiers," in *Holistic Mission. God's Plan for God's People*, ed. Brian Woolnough and Wonsuk Ma (Oxford: Regnum, 2010), 119–27.

[114] James F. Engel and William A. Dyrness, *Changing the Mind of Missions: Where Have We Gone Wrong?* (Downers Grove, IL: IVP, 2000), 93.

The last option is *radical liberation*, the typical representative of which is the Latin American liberation theologian Gustavo Gutiérrez. It identifies biblical salvation (*shalom*) with the struggle of the poor and marginalized for liberty and justice. The biblical model usually cited is the liberation of the people of Israel from Egyptian slavery.

Wrogemann and Hesselgrave's typologies are complementary and sum up effectively the historical development of the relationship between evangelism and social responsibility from a dichotomizing to a holistic perspective. We will return to their syntheses in chapter 3.

## Multiple Witness

So far, I have dealt with the relationship between evangelism and social action only in the Lausanne Movement. We can summarize it by means of the concept of the *two mandates*, creational and missionary, or the pairing of *word and deed*. I have not yet presented other propositions for a "multiple witness": the triple office or mission, the fourfold mission or fourfold mandate, and the five marks of mission.

Extending the pair of word and deed, the Micah Declaration speaks of the triad *being, doing, and saying*. John Calvin introduced another triad, the *threefold office* of Christ as prophet, priest, and king.[115] With the necessary distinctions between Jesus' and the disciples' mission, one can create a link between the triple office of Christ and the mission of the Church. According to this scheme, the Church's mission is threefold: worship of God, the priest's office (*leiturgia*), prophetic witness (*martyria*), and the king's service (*diakonia*). Willem Visser't Hooft, General Secretary of the WCC in the 1960s, replaced the vertical dimension in the triad, the worship of God (*leiturgia*), by a horizontal dimension, the fellowship of the saints (*koinonia*).[116] Johannes Hoekendijk modified the threefold scheme of Christian witness into service (*diakonia*), fellowship (*koinonia*) and preaching (*kerygma*), putting service in the first position as the "center of social integration" and proclamation last as the "optional explicative function."[117]

Based on this triple scheme and Visser't Hooft's and Hoekendijk's modifications, a formula for a *fourfold mission* of the Church has been developed that appears very often in the ecumenical movement. The New Affirmation of the WCC on mission and evangelism, *Together towards Life* (2012),

---

[115] John Calvin, *Institution of the Christian Religion*, II, 15.
[116] Willem A. Visser't Hooft, "Jesus Is Lord: The Kingship of Christ in the Bible," *Theology Today* vol. 4, no. 2 (1947): 177–89.
[117] Cf. Johannes Hoekendijk, *The Church Inside Out* (London: SCM, 1967).

formulates it in this way: "The Spirit calls us all towards an understanding of evangelism, which is grounded in the life of the local church where worship (*leiturgia*) is inextricably linked to witness (*martyria*), service (*diakonia*), and fellowship (*koinonia*).[118]

Esther Mombo, a Kenyan theologian and professor of the history of mission, perceives another form of fourfold mission in the missionary societies that served Africa during the nineteenth and twentieth centuries. According to her, it includes evangelism, education, medicine, and practical training, with evangelism for the purpose of conversion being placed first.[119] This arrangement seems to overlook agriculture, which was also very important in the African missionary enterprise.

Evert van de Poll's proposed *fourfold missionary mandate* is also interesting.[120] Using the overarching notion of witness, Van de Poll speaks of personal witness (which he calls discipleship), communitarian witness (of the Church), witness in words (proclamation), and witness in acts (service). Our sending by Jesus Christ, which he calls the "mission of God," underlies all four mandates. Although the labels chosen by van de Poll are not all fully clear, the underlying idea is rather convincing.

Another proposed version of multiple witness is the *Five Marks of mission* of the Anglican Communion:

1. To proclaim the good news of the Kingdom;
2. To teach, baptize and nurture new believers;
3. To respond to human need by loving service;
4. To seek to transform unjust structures of society;
5. To strive to safeguard the integrity of creation and sustain and renew the life of the earth.[121]

For the Anglican Communion, the Five Marks are not a final and complete statement on mission, but they offer a practical guide to the holistic nature

---

[118] Mission and Evangelism Commission of the World Council of Churches, *Together towards Life: Mission and Evangelism in Changing Landscapes: A New WCC Affirmation on Mission and Evangelism* (Geneva: WCC, 2013), paragraph 85.

[119] Esther Mombo, "From Fourfold Mission to Holistic Mission: Towards Edinburgh 2010," in Woolnough and Ma, *Holistic Mission*, 37–46.

[120] Evert van de Poll, "Témoignage multiple. La mission intégrale en quatre mandats," in *Mission intégrale: Vivre, annoncer et manifester l'Évangile pour que le monde croie* (Charols: Excelsis, 2017), 59–84.

[121] Andrew Walls and Cathy Ross (eds.), "The Five Marks of Mission," in *Mission in the 21st Century: Exploring the Five Marks of Global Mission* (London: Darton, Longman and Todd, 2008), 1–104; Christopher Wright, *The Five Marks of Mission* (London: Impress, 2015).

of mission, or a sort of checklist. They were first developed as four marks by the Anglican Consultative Council in 1984 and completed in 1990 with the addition of the fifth mark on safeguarding creation. Finally, the fourth mark was revised in 2012. The Anglican Communion considers the Five Marks as open to further amendment but as suitable to lead Anglican communities toward a self-understanding as mission-centered.[122] Cathy Ross explains: "The Five Marks are neither a perfect nor a complete definition of mission. They do not say everything we might want to say about mission in today's world. ... However, they do form a good working basis for a holistic approach to mission."[123]

Up to this point, the Five Marks of mission seem to be the most complete formulation of a multiple witness by including proclamation, discipleship, service, socio-political transformation, and ecological commitment. All these efforts to go beyond the pair of evangelism and social action indicate a tendency toward a more holistic conception of mission. However, the concept of multiple witness seems to be preferred by Global North theologians, who are accustomed to making distinctions with a dichotomizing worldview and a rule-centered conscience orientation. I will come back to this observation in the next section, where I continue these reflections with an in-depth analysis on the level of worldview, and in chapter 3.

## Evangelism and Mission in the Perspective of Worldview

In this section, I outline conclusions drawn from the analysis of the evangelical declarations presented in the first chapter, and I compare them to the development of worldviews on the various continents. I start with a brief recapitulation of the development of worldviews in the Lausanne Movement. Then I analyze the transformation of worldviews in the West from modernity to late modernity so as to situate the transformation of worldviews as observed in the evangelical declarations in the general context of the Global North. Finally, I review the worldviews of contextual theologies produced in the Global South, so as to place the phenomenon of holistic worldviews in its larger context.

---

[122] Anglican Communion, "History of the Five Marks of Mission," https://www.anglicancommunion.org/mission/marks-of-mission/history.aspx.

[123] Cathy Ross, "Introduction," in Walls and Ross, *Mission in the 21st Century*, xiv.

## Development of Worldviews in the Lausanne Movement

When we reviewed evangelical declarations in the first chapter, we observed John Stott's development of the concept of mission and of the relationship between evangelism and social responsibility. At Wheaton (1966), social action was for him not part of the Church's mission. He conceived of mission as a synonym for evangelism. This was evidently a dichotomizing perspective. After having met Latin American and African theologians with their holistic worldviews in his ministry with IFES, John Stott revised his conception at subsequent congresses and consultations, integrating social responsibility into a broader notion of mission while retaining a narrow concept of evangelism as a verbal approach. From then on, he saw evangelism and social responsibility as part of the "Christian duty." He preserved, however, the priority of evangelism in order to honor the Bible's insistence on human beings' eternal destiny, thereby maintaining a certain dichotomy.

The beginning of the twenty-first century has seen Christianity's transfer of the center of gravity in an advanced stage. The theologians of the Global South now represent the majority of global evangelicalism. As a consequence, their holistic worldview predominates in the Lausanne Movement and in the World Evangelical Alliance. Under the initiative of Global South theologians, who formulated the alternative declaration of Lausanne and founded the Micah Network, and of Stott's successor Christopher Wright, later declarations have expressed a holistic worldview and have introduced the notion of integral or holistic mission into the Lausanne texts. The holistic worldview manifests itself in the references by the alternative declaration of Lausanne (1974) and the Cape Town Commitment (2010) to spiritual warfare, reintroducing into the Lausanne texts the "middle sphere" excluded by the dichotomizing worldview.[124] It was interesting to hear Ruth Padilla de Borst note in an interview in 2014 that she sees two currents in the Lausanne Movement: "One that is much more pragmatic, strategist, managerial mission. And another one that is in my estimation deeper theologically, and I would also say more humble and more holistic. And those two strands, they were evident in 1974."[125]

---

[124] Paul G. Hiebert, "The Flaw of the Excluded Middle," *Missiology: An International Review* 10, no. 1 (1982): 35–47.

[125] Interview with Ruth Padilla de Borst on December 4, 2014, related by David C. Kirkpatrick, *A Gospel for the Poor: Global Social Christianity and the Latin American Evangelical Left* (Philadelphia: University of Pennsylvania Press, 2019), 158.

## Development of Worldviews from Modernity to Late Modernity

Parallel to the development of the debates in the Lausanne Movement, we can see in Europe, and with some differences in North America, a transformation of worldviews toward a more holistic approach—a tendency that has also influenced the theological and missiological perspectives of the evangelical declarations.

The changes that occurred in Europe during the Renaissance, the Reformation, the Enlightenment, and industrialization, a period generally called modern times or modernity, have favored a secular and fragmented worldview. During this period, Europeans were increasingly inclined to value efficacy, accomplishment, and punctuality. The importance of philosophy and science favored analytic thought. By generalizing (in the logic of a Weberian ideal type), we can say that modernity produces a type of person oriented toward efficacy and reason and with a dichotomizing or secular worldview.

In the framework of Christendom and neo-Platonism, the Church maintained a dichotomizing worldview. This worldview expressed itself in a separation of the spiritual and material domains and in a fragmented conception of salvation, limited to the salvation of the soul. The evangelical missionary movement of the nineteenth and twentieth centuries concentrated its efforts accordingly on the conversion of souls. However, in daily practice the missionaries included in their ministry a response to the immediate human needs of the people they served.

During the second half of the twentieth century, a new current appeared, which is called postmodernity, hypermodernity, or late modernity depending on the scientist's discipline and perspective.[126] The debate over the interpretation of this new current is still continuing. According to philosophers and sociologists, it is a radicalization, an acceleration, or a crisis of modernity. On the other hand, psychologists and anthropologists perceive an in-depth transformation of the functioning of people, or postmodernity as a counter-current to modernity. The French philosopher Luc Ferry observes three reactions to this crisis of modernity that he interprets as defining currents of late modernity. First, he sees a return to a premodern tradition. From a theological perspective, this represents an "orthodox" reaction into which part of the evangelical movement fits. Second, he sees an attempt at deconstruction, for example in Jacques Derrida and

---

[126] See for example Gilles Lipovetsky, *Hypermodern Times* (Cambridge: Polity Press, 2005).

Thomas Altizer, and third, an attempt of reconstruction. From a theological or ecclesiological perspective, one could classify here process theology and the movements of the Emerging or Missional Church.[127] Concerning the positioning of evangelicals in the reaction to this crisis, the French sociologists of religion Jean-Pierre Bastian, Françoise Champion, and Kathy Rousselet make an interesting observation:

> The evangelical orientation ... presents the apparent paradox of constituting a powerful reactive pole to a certain cultural modernity and to the homogenizing globalization, at the same time being perfectly in phase with the new modes of communication, which permit its global development and are precisely one of the most important factors of homogenization.[128]

This observation leads us to consider the effects of globalization on this development, especially as late modernity has developed hand in hand with the emergence of globalization. The most current interpretations of the impact of globalization on culture are the homogenization, fragmentation, and hybridization theories.[129]

*Homogenization theories* imply that globalization makes cultures more and more alike. To describe this phenomenon, George Ritzer introduced the expression of the "McDonaldization" of society.[130] In the same vein, Neal Blough (in personal communication) has referred to the "gospel of McDo, Disney and Facebook" to signify the uniformity of thought, the cult of efficacy and profitability, the cultural dominance by the entertainment sector, and the importance of appearances.

*Fragmentation theories* imply that globalization increases cross-cultural differences, tensions, and conflicts. Samuel Huntington's book *The Clash of Civilizations* (1997) is probably the best-known example of this perspective.[131] With regard to contextual theologies, many fear the fragmentation of theology into multiple local theologies: do we risk reaching a point where Asian, African or Latin American theologies do not have anything in common anymore?

---

[127] Luc Ferry, *Homo æstheticus. L'invention du goût à l'âge démocratique* (Paris: Grasset, 1990), 311–19.

[128] Jean-Pierre Bastian, Françoise Champion, and Kathy Rousselet, "La globalisation du religieux: diversité des questionnements et des enjeux," in *La globalisation du religieux* (Paris: l'Harmattan, 2001), 16.

[129] Cf. for example Craig Ott, "Globalization and Contextualization: Reframing the Task of Contextualization in the Twenty-First Century," *Missiology* 43, no. 1 (2015): 43–58.

[130] George Ritzer, *The McDonaldization of Society* (Thousand Oaks, CA: Pine Forge, 1993).

[131] Samuel P. Huntington, *The Clash of Civilizations and the Remaking of World Order* (New York: Free Press, 1997).

There is of course an element of truth in each theory, but the majority of authors claim that the two theories are simplistic. Roland Robertson comments:

> It is not a question of either homogenization or heterogenization, but rather of the ways in which both of these two tendencies have become features of life across much of the late-twentieth-century world. In this perspective, the problem becomes that of spelling out the ways in which homogenizing and heterogenizing tendencies are mutually implicative. … There are ongoing, calculated attempts to combine homogeneity with heterogeneity and universalism with particularism.[132]

French sociologist of religion Chantal Saint-Blancat reinforces Robertson's idea:

> Globalization is not a linear but a dialectic phenomenon, which structures itself in a complex manner around a global/local axis. … According to the *cultural theory* of Roland Robertson, globalization does not introduce homogeneity, but a multiple hybridity, a relativization of identities, which allows for a reconciliation of universalism and particularism. It is not a simple adaptation but a complex process wherein universal religious models transform themselves upon contact with differentiated cultural and religious systems and acquire their own autonomy.[133]

Robertson suggests the term "glocalization" to describe this mix of global and local, of global homogenization and affirmation of local identities. However, the majority of authors call this mix "hybridity," among them Chantal Saint-Blancat, William Burrows, Daniel Shaw, and Jan Nederveen Pieterse.[134] Nederveen Pieterse remarks, "Hybridity has become a regular, almost ordinary fixture in popular and mainstream culture, widely recognized as 'The Trend to Blend.'"[135]

The current of late modernity presents itself in many different ways that have links to globalization, fragmentation, and hybridization. We

---

[132] Roland Robertson, "Glocalization: Time-Space and Homogeneity-Heterogeneity," in *Global Modernities*, ed. M. Featherstone, S. Lash, and R. Robertson (Thousand Oaks, CA: Sage, 1995), 27.

[133] Chantal Saint-Blancat, "Globalisation, réseaux et diasporas," in Bastian, Champion, and Rousselet, *La globalisation du religieux*, 75, 77.

[134] R. Daniel Shaw, "Beyond Syncretism: A Dynamic Approach to Hybridity," *International Bulletin of Mission Research* 42, no. 1 (2018): 6–19; Jan Nederveen Pieterse, *Globalization and Culture: Global Mélange*, 2nd ed. (New York: Rowman & Littlefield, 2009).

[135] Nederveen Pieterse, *Globalization and Culture*, viii.

must realize that the concepts of modernity and late modernity are complex and fuzzy. We must also keep in mind that during times of cultural change, elements of continuity and discontinuity exist side by side. Depending on one's main perspective on continuity or discontinuity, a divergence in points of view should not be surprising.[136] Orientation toward accomplishment, individualism, analytical thinking, and a fragmented worldview indicate a continuation of the characteristics of modernity. On the other hand, psychologists and anthropologists have observed a transition from a dichotomizing worldview in the generations born before and after World War II toward a relational and holistic worldview in contemporary generations.[137] On the one side, we are inclined to speak of the continuation of the characteristics of modernity, and on the other side of a new epoch with a relational functioning and a holistic worldview. However, even during modernity the personality profiles in society were a mixture. Since the hybridization of societies and the large migratory movements, the mixture and the relational tendency have increased, because the majority of migrants have a relational functioning and a holistic worldview.

With the young generations and the migrants in the West tending toward a relational and holistic worldview, the proposals of holistic definitions of mission coming from theologians from the Global North are not surprising anymore. However, these are not generally accepted because during this cultural change, certain theologians still prefer a dichotomizing conception of mission. At the same time, it would be naïve to think that cultures are homogeneous and that all members of a given

---

[136] This interpretation of late modernity as a cultural transformation corresponds to the fifth option proposed by French sociologist Yves Bonny. According to him, late modernity can be interpreted as (1) an aesthetic sensitivity, (2) a state of mind, (3) a set of philosophical and epistemological orientations, (4) a set of moral and political positions, or (5) a cultural mutation. Yves Bonny, *Sociologie du temps présent. Modernité avancée ou postmodernité?* (Paris: Armand Colin, 2004), 65–89.

[137] This is the theory of generations, which distinguishes a sequence of different generations from a sociological perspective, first in American society and subsequently elsewhere. For a secular analysis, see for example William Strauss and Neil Howe, *Generations: The History of America's Future, 1584 to 2069* (New York: Quill, 1992). For an analysis of Generation X, see Douglas Coupland, *Generation X: Tales for Accelerated Culture* (London: Abacus, 1996). For a missiological perspective, see Kath Donovan and Ruth Myors, "A Generational Perspective into the Future," in *Too Valuable to Lose: Exploring the Causes and Cures of Missionary Attrition*, ed. William D. Taylor (Pasadena, CA: William Carey Library, 1997) 41–73, synoptic table on p. 48; James E. White, *Meet Generation Z. Understanding and Reaching the New Post-Christian World* (Grand Rapids, MI: Baker, 2017).

culture have the same conscience orientation and the same worldview. The basic layers of worldview are formed in the socialization process during early childhood. Worldviews are thus different from individual to individual. Consequently, it is necessary to exercise caution in making generalizations.

Having studied the missiological debates in the Lausanne Movement and the parallel development of worldviews in the Global North, let us now inquire into the worldviews underlying the contextual theologies produced in the Global South, so as to situate the positions of those theologians in the missiological debates of the Lausanne Movement in a larger context.

## Worldviews Underlying the Contextual Theologies of the Global South

In the debates over the relationship between evangelism and social responsibility in the Lausanne Movement, we have observed that the worldview of the theologians from the Global South is mostly holistic. Their holistic worldview has left its mark on the intra-evangelical debate. We will consider now whether this holistic worldview manifests itself also in the contextual theologies of the Global South produced by these theologians.

I have already mentioned that Latin American Catholics and evangelicals were not satisfied with the Western "salvation of souls" approach. The former have developed a more holistic approach that accounts for the needs of their context, called liberation theology. As a response to this same context and to liberation theology, Latin American evangelicals developed the concept of integral mission during the early discussions of the Latin American Theological Fraternity.[138]

African theologians, such as Engelbert Mveng and Jean-Marc Éla, have shown a keen interest in the holistic approach of liberation theology, but have adapted it to their context. In their "inculturation theologies," an entirely holistic approach, the African theologians integrate the relationships to the invisible world—particularly the ancestors, regulators of daily life—and to nature, which represents the context that determines the success of their life.[139]

---

[138] Cf. Samuel Escobar, "Latin American Theology," in *Dictionary of Mission Theology: Evangelical Foundations*, ed. John Corrie, Samuel Escobar, and Wilbert Shenk (Downers Grove, IL: IVP, 2007), 203–7.

[139] Cf. Bénézet Bujo, *African Theology in its Social Context* (Nairobi: St. Paul-Africa, 1992).

Asian theologians have also been interested in liberation theology with its consideration of the context and its holistic approach. Living in a context of monist religions in search of cosmic harmony, they often speak of the cosmic Christ by analogy to the cosmic Buddha, as does for example Bishop K. H. Ting of the Chinese Three-Self Patriotic Movement. Adopting a holistic approach in their theologies, several Indian theologians seek to create harmony between Christianity and Hinduism, the religion of their context. This is for example the case for M. M. Thomas and Stanley J. Samartha, both former general secretaries of the WCC.[140]

Based on this very brief overview, we can conclude provisionally that most southern theologians of Catholic, ecumenical or evangelical orientation have developed their contextual theologies based on a holistic worldview, the basic worldview of their contexts. We have already noted this fact in our discussions of the Lausanne Movement. Evangelical theologians and missiologists, however, generally introduced biblical distinctions into their contextual holism. Logically, the theologians from the Global South criticize those from the Global North for their dichotomizing worldview. While acknowledging that his generalization represents a gross simplification, David Bosch perceives four general tendencies in the Western approach: a dichotomizing worldview, a one-sided spirituality, intellectualism and individualism. He characterizes the dichotomizing worldview in this way: "The soul remains opposed to the body, redemption to creation, the word to the deed, evangelism to social action, the invisible to the visible, the abstract to the concrete, the sacred to the secular, theology to ethics and religion to society."[141]

This dichotomizing and fragmentary worldview influences spirituality and theology: being saved is perceived as an exclusively spiritual experience, as opposed to a holistic perception including the physical and social aspects of salvation. This worldview also favors Western intellectualism, which conceives of faith as cognitive, conceptual, and propositional (orthodoxy), rather than from an experiential and participative perspective (orthopraxy).

How can we arrive at a balance, a theology that is not only contextual but also universal? Here is what Bosch proposes:

> What we are in need of, therefore, is creative interaction between different "local" theologies, in the first and third worlds. In that way we may tentatively

---

[140] Cf. Timoteo D. Gener and Stephen D. Pardue (eds.), *Asian Christian Theology: Evangelical Perspectives* (Carlisle, UK: Langham Global Library, 2019).

[141] David Bosch, "An Emerging Paradigm for Mission," *Missiology* 11, no. 4 (1983): 498; for a discussion of the four tendencies, see 497–501.

advance towards a truly "catholic" theology, which is not to be a new monolithic superstructure, but a "zone" in which we can communicate creatively with one another. Once again, it is only "together with all God's people" that we shall discover how broad and long, how high and deep Christ's love is.[142]

To Bosch's proposal, I would add that we all particularly need a faithful anchoring in the biblical record and an understanding of the influence of our worldview upon our theologizing and, in consequence, the contingency of our theological productions.

Having studied the missiological debates in the Lausanne Movement and the development of worldviews in different continents, we have observed, on one hand, a parallel transformation of worldviews in the Lausanne Movement and in the larger context of the Global North during the passage from modernity to late modernity and globalization. This development reflects, generally speaking, the transformation of a dichotomizing and rules-centered worldview into a holistic and relational one. An influence of the larger context on theological production seems evident. On the other hand, we noted a generally holistic worldview in the contextual theologies produced in the Global South. Let us now inquire as to what the Bible says about the definition of evangelism and mission.

## Evangelism and Mission in the Bible

As we have seen in the missiological debates and in the discussion on worldview, theologians and missiologists define the notions of evangelism and mission differently, influenced by their worldview. Following the logic of modern philosophical linguistics, which affirms that language is a play of words with haphazard conventions, one can say with Ludwig Wittgenstein, "Say what you want, if it does not hinder you from seeing what there is."[143] This issue reminds us of the conversation between the English characters of fiction, Alice in Wonderland and Humpty Dumpty:

> "When I use a word," Humpty Dumpty said in a rather scornful tone, "it means just what I choose it to mean, neither more nor less." "The question is," said Alice, "whether you can make words mean different things." "The question is," said Humpty Dumpty, "which is to be master—that's all."[144]

---

[142] Bosch, "An Emerging Paradigm for Mission," 501.
[143] Ludwig Wittgenstein, *Philosophical Investigations*, 2nd ed., trans. G. Anscombe (Oxford: Blackwell, 1972), § 79.
[144] Lewis Carroll, *Through the Looking-Glass* (Raleigh, NC: Hayes Barton Press, 1872), 72. *Through the Looking-Glass* was Carroll's sequel to *Alice in Wonderland* (1865).

But as David Hesselgrave warns, "A flawed hermeneutic and sub-orthodox view of Scripture allows for a definitional free-for-all in which terms can be redefined without regard for the clear intention of the biblical authors, in which case the world, not the kingdom, sets the agenda."[145]

For example, "mission" has been variously described as building the kingdom of God, establishing *shalom*, humanization, participation in the *missio Dei* (God's mission), or everything the church does. But as Anglican bishop Stephen Neill commented, "If everything is mission, nothing is mission."[146] John Stott, speaking at the first Lausanne Congress in 1974, also evoked a situation akin to *Alice in Wonderland*:

> The issue between Alice and Humpty Dumpty—whether man can manipulate the meaning of words or whether words have an autonomy, which cannot be infringed—is still a contemporary issue. "The modern church sometimes seems like a kind of theological wonderland in which numerous Humpty Dumptys enjoy playing with words and making them mean what they want them to mean. ... I shall try to define [the meaning of the words] according to Scripture."[147]

Like Stott, we want to ask how the Bible understands the missionary terms. For us evangelicals, Scripture is the point of reference for all questions of faith and life. In an effort to resolve the confusion, I present here a biblical study of key words and concepts related to our being sent on mission and the communication of the gospel. I begin with those terms that one can classify in dichotomizing categories and then discuss those that imply a holistic view of mission. After that, I apply this biblical analysis to current perspectives, including various notions of mission and salvation that are expressed in contemporary missiology.

## Biblical Terms of the Semantic Domains of Sending and Communication

In the Bible, the notion of "mission" occurs in the form of the verb "to send" (Hebrew *shalah*, Greek *apostellō* and *pempō*). The concept of sending is very common in both testaments: God sends the patriarchs and the prophets (Gen 6:18; 12:1; Ex 3:10; Isa 6:9; Jer 2:2; Ezek 3:1; Jon 1:2), and "when the times were fulfilled, God has sent his Son" (Gal 4:4; Jn 3:16). The Son sends his disciples (Mt 10:5; Lk 9:2; 10:1), just as he has been sent (Jn

---

[145] Hesselgrave, *Paradigms in Conflict*, 346.
[146] Stephen C. Neill, *Creative Tension* (London: Edinburgh House, 1959), 81.
[147] John Stott, "Biblical Basis of Evangelism," in Douglas, *Let the Earth Hear His Voice*, 65f.

17:18; 20:21). The sending of the disciples *par excellence* takes place before Jesus' ascension and is confirmed in the final texts of the gospels and in the beginning of the book of Acts, in what we call the Great Commission (Mt 28:18-20; Mk 16:15-18; Lk 24:44-49; Jn 20:21; Acts 1:8). The sending always implies the functions of witness (Isa 43:10, 12; Rev 1:5; 11:3, 7) and ambassador (2 Cor 5:20). This fact clarifies the relationship between "mission" (sending) and "evangelism": generally speaking, Jesus was sent to "evangelize" (*euangelizomai*), to be a witness (*martys*), to call, gather and send his disciples (*mathēteuō*) and to serve (*diakoneō*). God's sending implies that each task is under his Kingdom rule; he specifies the task by his call. This close biblical link between the sending and the task explains why in contemporary terminology "mission" not only means "sending" but also includes all kinds of activities in the semantic domain of the "communication of the gospel."

The expression "preach the gospel" (or "proclaim the gospel," Greek *keryssō to euangelion*, e.g., Mk 1:38; 16:15), is used on one hand to denote a verbal activity and on the other hand for the total ministry of Jesus and the apostles.[148] The latter sense can be assumed when *keryssō* does not occur in parallel or in opposition to a verbal activity. Goldsworthy interprets *keryssō* also in this sense when it occurs in parallel to *euangelizomai*, for example when used in the Septuagint of Isaiah 61:1: "This eschatological proclamation is the means to obtain liberation and liberty. This proclamation is an integral part of the ministry of Jesus (Mk 1:38; Lk 4:18-19, quoting Isa 61:1-2 and Lk 4:43-44, which links *euangelizomai* and *keryssein*)."[149]

In the missionary mandate of the gospel of Matthew, Jesus commands his disciples to teach (*didaskō*) the nations "to obey everything that I have commanded you" (Mt 28:20). Jesus not only preaches but teaches everywhere he goes (Lk 23:5). He is known as a teacher (Jn 3:2, 10). The same qualifications of preacher and teacher are attributed to the apostle Paul (Acts 21:28; 2 Tim 1:11). It seems evident that teaching is a process of verbal communication. However, does teaching limit itself to words? Does the fact that Jesus gathers the disciples around him before sending them (Mk 3:13-15) not imply a more encompassing pedagogical process?

---

[148] See the occurrences of *keryssō to euangelion* in the sense of verbal proclamation of the gospel: Mt 4:23 (preach the gospel and heal); Mt 26:13 (preach and tell); Mk 1:14f (preach and say); 1:38f (preach and cast out demons); 13:10f (preach and say); see also 1 Thess 2:2 (*laleō* "say the gospel"), and in the sense of the total ministry of Jesus and the apostles, Mt 24:14 and parallels; Mk 16:15; see also Acts 20:24 (witness the gospel).

[149] Graeme L. Goldsworthy, "Gospel," in *New Dictionary of Biblical Theology*, ed. B. Rosner and T. Alexander (Leicester, UK: IVP, 2000), 577.

The biblical use of the verb "evangelize" (*euangelizomai*) also allows for two interpretations, both of which we find among evangelical theologians. On one hand, *euangelizomai* can denote verbal proclamation of the gospel.[150] From this point of view, evangelism has priority over social action because it deals with the eternal destiny of man. Advocates of this approach distinguish evangelism from mission, which in this view usually includes all verbal and non-verbal activities related to the proclamation and the presentation of the gospel. On the other hand, *euangelizomai* can denote all the activities of Jesus' and the apostles' ministry, including all aspects of the communication of the gospel, not limited to verbal proclamation.[151] This second interpretation encompasses the first. In this interpretation, evangelism is synonymous with the notions of "making disciples" and of "mission." From this point of view, the eternal destiny of man has the priority independently of whether a verbal or a non-verbal activity is involved. The first interpretation is the traditional evangelical position and that of the Lausanne Movement before the turn of the millennium; the second is that of the Cape Town Commitment and the Micah Network. The second interpretation encompasses the first and leads to the notion of integral or holistic mission.

According to the reader's worldview, he or she will interpret occurrences provided here for the total ministry of Jesus and the apostles in the sense of verbal proclamation, and others will see in occurrences given for

---

[150] For the verbal proclamation of the gospel, see the following occurrences of *euangelizomai*: Lk 4:43 (parallel to preach in v. 44); Lk 9:6 (evangelize and heal); Lk 20:1 and Acts 5:42 (teach and evangelize); Acts 8:4 and 15:35 ("evangelize" the word); Acts 8:25 (witness, say and evangelize); Acts 8:35 (open the mouth and evangelize); Acts 10:36 (announce peace); Acts 11:20 (say and evangelize); Acts 13:32 (announce the gospel of promise); Rom 10:15 (parallel between preaching, sending and evangelizing); 1 Cor 1:17 (contrast with baptize); 1 Cor 15:1 ("evangelize" the gospel); Gal 1:8 (parallel to preach); Heb 4:2 and 1 Pet 1:25 (parallel with the word).

[151] For the total ministry of Jesus and the apostles, see the following occurrences of *euangelizomai*: Mt 11:5 and Lk 4:18–19 (if one considers the sequence of mentioned actions as a synonymic parallelism); Lk 16:16; Acts 14:7; 16:10; Rom 10:15 (parallel between preaching, sending and evangelizing); Rom 15:20; 1 Cor 9:16, 18; 2 Cor 10:16; 11:7; Gal 1:8, 11, 16, 23; 4:13; Eph 2:17; 3:8. For an argument in favor of an interpretation of the notion of "proclamation of the gospel" in the sense of the total ministry of Jesus and the apostles, see Stott, *Christian Mission in the Modern World*, 25–87; Ulrich Becker, "Gospel, Evangelize, Evangelist," in *New International Dictionary of the New Testament*, vol. 2, ed. Colin Brown, rev. ed. (Carlisle, UK: Paternoster; Grand Rapids, MI: Zondervan, 1986), 111, 113. Becker supports this interpretation particularly in relation to Paul's use of *euangelizomai*.

the verbal proclamation an implicit indication of their whole ministry. For example, there are two ways to interpret Jesus' sermon at Nazareth (Lk 4:18f). *Euangelizomai* can be seen in opposition to the other components of Jesus' ministry as healing the brokenhearted, releasing the captives, providing recovery of sight and liberating the bruised. This point of view suggests an interpretation in the sense of verbal communication. On the other hand, *euangelizomai* together with this spectrum of activities can indicate Jesus' whole ministry in the logic of a synonymic parallelism. The same two options appear in Jesus' answer to the disciples of John the Baptist: *euangelizomai* can be seen as distinct from or as encompassing the acts of healing the blind, the lame, the lepers, and the deaf (Mt 11:5; Lk 7:22). Moreover, the majority of the occurrences classified in favor of the total ministry of Jesus and the apostles, for example because *euangelizomai* has no object, can according to the worldview of the reader be equally interpreted in the sense of a verbal activity. In this vein, one can interpret *euangelizomai* in Romans 15:20 in the sense of the verbal proclamation of the gospel as well as the total ministry of the apostle Paul.

We continue with two terms that denote an action: "heal" (*therapeuō*) and "cast out demons" (*ekballō ta daimonia*). They can denote the simple act of healing and casting out demons (Mt 8:13, 16; 12:15, 22; 14:14; 15:30; 19:2; 21:14 and parallels; Mk 1:34; 16:17f; Lk 14:4; Acts 3:6; 10:38). They are often used in opposition to a term denoting a verbal activity. For example, it is said of God that he "sent out his word and healed (*rafa'*) them" (Ps 107:20). Jesus preaches the gospel of the kingdom, casts out demons, and heals (Mt 4:23f; 9:32f). And he sends his disciples to preach, heal, and cast out demons (Mt 10:7f; Mk 3:14f; 16:15, 17).

The situation is a little more complex for the term "serve" (*diakoneō*), which in English clearly denotes a social, non-verbal activity. In allusion to the "Servant of the Lord" (*'ebed yhwh*) of Isaiah 42–53, service carries a more general sense. In this vein, Jesus says, "I am among you as one who serves" (Lk 22:27), and "Just as the Son of Man came not to be served but to serve, and to give his life a ransom for many" (Mt 20:28; Mk 10:45). Service is here linked with the propitiatory sacrifice of the Servant of the Lord. Later on, the notion extends to the general ministry of the apostles, such as Paul: "I am on my way to Jerusalem in the service of the Lord's people there" (Rom 15:25). For him and his collaborators, the term can denote the overall work of ministry (*diakonia*: 2 Cor 8:19; 1 Tim 3:10, 13; 1 Pet 1:12; 4:10).

The task given to Jesus' disciples, or in other words their service (ministry), is "to make disciples" (*mathēteuō*, Mt 28:19). This is according to Jesus' example of calling the disciples around him in order to send them (Mk 3:13–15). This process of sharing common life during a period of several years implies a process of transformation with many verbal and non-verbal pedagogical components. As the Father has sent the Son, Jesus sends his disciples (Jn 17:18; 20:21) to repeat this pedagogical process with others (Mt 28:19). To make disciples is apparently an integral ministry.

The verb "to witness" (*martyreō*) and notions of "being a witness" (*eimi martys*) or of witness itself (*martyria*) are equally a matter of the total person. This is certainly one reason why these notions are very much present in the Cape Town Commitment. Another reason is that they do not carry the heavy theological baggage that the terms "evangelism" and "mission" do. The people of Israel had been called to be a witness (*'ed*) for God, his uniqueness, and his liberating acts (Isa 43:10, 12; 44:8). The Servant of the Lord is the witness *par excellence* (Isa 43:10; 55:4). Following him, Jesus is the witness to the truth (Jn 18:37), the "faithful witness" (Rev 1:5). Witness is also at the center of the two Lukan missionary mandates:

> And he said to them, "Thus it is written, that the Messiah is to suffer and to rise from the dead on the third day, and that repentance and forgiveness of sins is to be proclaimed in his name to all nations, beginning from Jerusalem. You are witnesses of these things." (Lk 24:46–48)
>
> But you will receive power when the Holy Spirit has come upon you; and you will be my witnesses in Jerusalem, in all Judea and Samaria, and to the ends of the earth. (Acts 1:8)

Peter and Paul, and the apostles in general, are witnesses to Jesus, his life, and his acts (Acts 2:32; 3:15; 5:32; 10:39; 22:15; 23:11; 1 Pet 5:1; Rev 11:3, 7; 17:6). It is astonishing that the notion of witness did not carry greater importance in missiology before the second half of the twentieth century. Concerning the witness of the Church, Lesslie Newbigin introduces the concept of an "ecclesiological hermeneutic" to underscore its importance and holistic character:

> The whole life of the church, understood correctly, is the visible means by which the Holy Spirit accomplishes His mission in the world, and thus the totality of the life of the church participates in her character of witness. The whole life of the church has thus a missionary dimension, even if it does not have mission as primary intention.[152]

---

[152] Lesslie Newbigin, *One Body, One Gospel, One World: The Christian Mission Today* (London and New York: International Missionary Council, 1958), 21.

Although the concept of mission includes several terms with either a dichotomizing or a holistic connotation, the Bible also uses metaphors to speak of the communication of the good news, usually in a holistic manner. I will mention four examples here.

First, the law prescribes *salt* as a means to conserve and flavor food to be part of the offerings. In this way, salt has become a symbol of the faithfulness and steadfastness of the covenants in the ancient Near East in general and of God's covenant with Israel in particular. In this perspective, the Old Testament speaks of the "salt of your God's covenant" (Lev 2:13; cf. Num 18:19; 2 Chron 13:5). Jesus is referring to this cultural background when he says of his disciples, "You are the salt of the earth; but if salt has lost its taste, how can its saltiness be restored?" (Mt 5:13).

Second, since ancient times, *light* has represented the presence and the favor of God (cf. Ps 27:2; Isa 9:2; 2 Cor 4:6). In the present context, it symbolizes the radiance of the good news. In this sense, the Servant of the Lord is called to be a light for the nations (Isa 42:6). Jesus, the Servant of the Lord *par excellence*, is himself the Light (Jn 1:4–9), and he charges the disciples to be the "light of the world" (Mt 5:14-16).

Interestingly, Henri Blocher takes a dichotomizing approach to the interpretation of these two metaphors. In his view, as the "salt of the earth," the disciples play the role of preserving God's creation from total ruin and reducing the perversion of the world through actions that honor God. As the "light of the world," they present the way of salvation with persuasion. In other words, the metaphor of salt refers to actions and light to words. As a logical consequence of this dichotomizing, Blocher identifies being light for the world as the top priority.[153]

The Bible mentions two other metaphors that indicate the radiance of the good news. First, Paul wrote, "You show that you are a *letter* of Christ ... written ... with the Spirit of the living God" (2 Cor 3:3). The Christians are also compared to a *fragrance* for their environment: "For we are to God the pleasing aroma of Christ among those who are being saved and those who are perishing. To the one we are an aroma that brings death; to the other, an aroma that brings life" (2 Cor 2:15f, NIV). Evidently, according to the Bible, these metaphors evoke Christian witness as a whole, verbal and non-verbal.

## Missiological Concepts in the Light of the Bible

Can we also find a basis for missiological models of multiple witness in the Bible? We have seen that the Bible presents sending ("mission") as an

---

[153] Henri Blocher, "La mission de l'Église," *Promesse* no. 186 (2013).

underlying element of all tasks involved in the communication of the good news. In this way, it distinguishes itself in a significant way from the contemporary usage of the term in the missiological debates of the Lausanne Movement, as a concept encompassing several modes of communication. On the other hand, the Bible presents "evangelism" as a term that can denote the verbal proclamation of the gospel, in continuity with the usage in the Lausanne Movement, but also as a term denoting the whole ministry of Jesus and the apostles, in discontinuity with the contemporary usage in the Lausanne Movement. Other biblical terms for mission can also denote the totality of communication, both verbal and non-verbal.

Concerning the two concepts of "evangelism" and "social action," according to Timothy Tennent, professor of missiology and president of Asbury Theological Seminary (USA), the Old Testament identifies three qualities of God's character:[154] justice (*mishpat*), loving kindness (*hesed*), and compassion (*rahamim*). God demonstrates them through his concern for four groups of persons: widows, orphans, immigrants, and the poor (Ex 22:21f; Ps 68:5; 82:3f; Isa 10:2; Jer 22:3). God's people have to reflect God's character. The evaluation of these three attitudes is found in people's behavior toward the marginalized on a personal level (Ex 22:27; Lev 19:9f; 23:22; Deut 24:19–21) and on a structural level (Ex 12:49; 23:2; Lev 24:22; Prov 29:14; Isa 10:1; Jer 22:16; Mal 3:5).

In the New Testament, Jesus is born into a poor family (Jn 1:46) and identifies himself with the poor and the marginalized. Luke-Acts demonstrates this fact especially strongly. In the Magnificat, Mary situates herself among the poor (Lk 1:52–53). Jesus announces the good news to the poor (Lk 4:18) and declares the poor blessed and honorable (Mt 5:3; Lk 6:20). This blessing places in tension the persons who are spiritually poor, i.e., those who consider themselves in need of God and his forgiveness (Mt 5:3), and those who are globally and materially poor (Lk 6:20). For Jesus, even the materially rich, and maybe especially the rich, can be spiritually blind or poor (Lk 12:16–21; 16:19–31). This identification with the poor, crippled, paralyzed, and blind is put in an eschatological context in the parable of the great banquet (Lk 14:13f; Mt 22:9f) and the parable of the sheep and the goats (Mt 25:31–46). Interestingly, in these passages, Jesus will receive those who will have been involved in social action! Beyond this identification with the poor, Jesus heals the sick as a sign of the kingdom of God to come (Lk 7:22; 11:20) and sends the disciples to do the same (Mt

---

[154] In this discussion, I follow Timothy C. Tennent, "Reflecting the Incarnation in Holistic Missions," in *Invitation to World Missions: A Trinitarian Missiology for the Twenty-first Century* (Grand Rapids: Zondervan, 2010), 387–406.

10:7f; Lk 9:1–6; 10:1–16). This eschatological perspective continues in the book of Acts in the ministry of the apostles: the paralyzed walk (Acts 3:1-10; 14:8–10), the blind see (Acts 9:1–18), and the doors of prisons open (Acts 5:19; 16:26). Here we see a predominance of non-verbal communication.

On the other hand, in many cases Jesus begins his proclamation of the good news of the kingdom with a call to repentance, starting with Mark 1:14f. The apostles continue this method of proclamation in the book of Acts, starting with Peter at Pentecost (Acts 2:38) and continuing with Paul who stated, "We preach Christ crucified" (1 Cor 1:23). These are instances of predominantly verbal communication of the gospel.

To sum up these observations, Tennent speaks of a "paradigm of evangelism" and of a "paradigm of social action." However, he notes, "Once evangelism and social action are conceptualized as two separate spheres, it is inevitable that evangelism is given a priority over social action."[155] The hermeneutical circle thus closes itself. A theologian with a dichotomizing worldview will tend to see separate concepts, make distinctions, and define priorities. In contrast, a theologian with a holistic worldview will see the whole and may not understand the relevance of distinctions. We can see this tension in the various ways in which people understand evangelism and mission. The notion of holistic or integral mission can finally lead to not making distinctions at all, as for example Bryant Myers and Ronald Sider seem to propose.[156] On the other hand, despite their generally holistic perspective, the Micah Declaration still distinguishes between evangelism and transformation, and the Cape Town Commitment distinguishes witness of truth from witness of life.

Tennent argues, from a holistic perspective, in favor of recognizing "the fundamental unity between word and deed."[157] He also urges that we "resist individualism that does not make room for various gifts and graces in the body of Christ."[158] From his holistic perspective, Tennent provides this definition of evangelism:

> [Evangelism] is not merely about discipling *individuals*; it is about our summoning the *entire culture* to the inbreaking realities of the New Creation. Evangelism is the permeation of the whole gospel into every aspect of a culture and demonstrating, through word and deed, what it means to be "in Christ." Evangelism is not just about our "doing"; it is fundamentally about our "being." The church is to be a community of health, demonstrating

---

[155] Tennent, "Reflecting the Incarnation," 393.
[156] Myers, "Holistic Mission: New Frontiers," 119–27; Sider, "Words and Deeds," 47.
[157] Tennent, "Reflecting the Incarnation," 399.
[158] Ibid., 403.

through our words and actions the qualities of justice (*mishpat*), kindness/faithfulness (*hesed*), and compassion (*rahamim*).[159]

For John Stott, writing here also from a holistic perspective, there are three reasons for the integration of the different dimensions of Christian witness.[160] The first deals with the character of God, who is both Creator and Redeemer. He is interested in the total well-being of man created in his image and wants him to live in abundance. In return, he demands a total allegiance from his people. Micah 6:8, the watchword of the Micah Network, expresses these imperatives well: "He has told you, O mortal, what is good; and what does the Lord require of you but to do justice (*mishpat*), and to love kindness (*hesed*), and to walk humbly with your God?" The first recommendation in this verse concerns the reciprocal relationship between human beings, the second indicates a proper attitude toward the needy, and the third involves our attitude towards our Creator. Understood in this way, Micah 6:8 encompasses all the situations of human life. The Law and the Prophets reveal God's character, and we should witness to him in the same holistic way.

The second reason for integration, according to Stott, deals with Jesus' ministry and teaching: "Jesus' words explained his actions, and the former eloquently demonstrated the latter. ... Words without acts lack credibility; acts without words lack clarity. Jesus' actions rendered his words visible; his words rendered his acts intelligible."[161] We find the same holistic approach in Jesus' teaching. As an illustration, Stott mentions the parables of the prodigal son (Lk 15:11–32) and the Good Samaritan (Lk 10:30–37). God does not want his creatures to get lost and lose courage, but he wants the lost and the wounded to come back. Both stories call for love and compassion. Both show that we have to make a choice. However, there are differences: the prodigal son is a victim of his own personal sin, and the Samaritan is a victim of the social sins of others.

The third reason for integration, according to Stott, relates to the communication of the gospel. Communication studies remind us that the most effective communication includes both verbal and non-verbal components.[162] Followers of Jesus should not neglect verbal witness, but we

---

[159] Ibid., 404–5, emphasis in the original.
[160] John Stott, "Holistic Mission," in Stott, *The Contemporary Christian: Applying God's Word to Today's World* (Downers Grove, IL: IVP, 1992), 343–49.
[161] Stott, "Holistic Mission," 346.
[162] Paul Watzlawick, Janet H. Helminck-Beavin, and Don D. Jackson, *Pragmatics of Human Communication: A Study of Interactional Patterns, Pathologies, and Paradoxes* (New York: W. W. Norton & Co., 1967).

should also render our words visible in our lives, just as God rendered his Word visible in Jesus Christ (Jn 1:14). Just as God shares our concerns, our suffering, and our struggles in Jesus, he calls us to enter into the social reality of our neighbors. Through this integration, our acts "become preaching," as Johan Bavinck says.[163]

## Conceptions of Mission and Salvation

Our worldview influences not only our theological and missiological positions, but also our biblical interpretations. This dynamic can be observed in the debate over where mission starts in the Bible. Several options have been proposed. They imply different conceptions of mission and salvation. I will start with the most traditional view and work backwards.

*Does mission start with Jesus Christ's propitiatory death* on the cross and his resurrection? The Protestant missionary movement of the nineteenth century adopted this approach, according to which the Great Commission of Matthew 28 carries supreme importance for mission. An important representative of this position, David Bosch, devoted just four of 500 pages in his 1991 book *Transforming Mission* to mission in the Old Testament. This option implies a relatively narrow definition of mission and salvation.

*Does mission start with the ministry of Jesus?* Luke 4:18–19 has frequently been cited in this way within the ecumenical movement, by radical evangelicals, and by the Micah Network. In Luke 4, the definition of mission and salvation is broad, including not only eternal salvation but also physical, social, and political aspects. However, these groups tend not to highlight the effusion of the Holy Spirit (v. 22) and the forgiveness of sins (v. 23). The parallel passage of John 20:21 is also quoted often by these circles and was emphasized by John Stott. Missiology has tended to neglect these two passages in the past.

*Does mission start with Abraham's sending* in Genesis 12? Abraham is blessed and mandated to be a blessing for all the families of the earth. The New Testament often refers to Abraham. The missionary mandates at the end of the gospels, however, are not mentioned in the epistles. The notion of blessing as stated in the Cape Town Commitment could encompass this creational and missionary mandate, to live and proclaim the truth (in the terminology of the Cape Town Commitment). In this way, the definitions of mission and salvation become broad. However, certain interpreters

---

[163] Johan H. Bavinck, *An Introduction to the Science of Missions* (Philadelphia: Presbyterian and Reformed, 1960), 113, quoted by Stott, "Holistic Mission," 349.

introduce a dichotomy between material and spiritual dimensions into the notion of blessing.

*Does mission start with the Fall* in Genesis 3? In this case, the objective would be the restoration of the relationship between God and mankind. The representatives of this option tend to distinguish clearly between the creational and the missionary mandate. This implies narrow definitions of mission and salvation.

*Does mission start with the declaration of biblical monotheism* in Genesis 1? A distinction between the creational and missionary mandate would become meaningless, or at least difficult to sustain, in this option. On the other hand, the notions of mission and salvation would become quite broad. This is the position of Christopher Wright, coordinator of the Theological Commission of the Lausanne Movement, in his 2006 book *The Mission of God*.

As for why someone may prefer one of these options, it seems that one's foundational worldview, which is mostly subconscious, may play a role. Each approach tends to base its theology of mission on one or two key verses. The approaches do not develop a theology of mission that draws on the missional dimension of the whole Bible, i.e., a missional hermeneutic of the Bible, as Christopher Wright recommends.[164]

After this overview of the possible starting points of mission in the Bible, we must ask which one would seem most appropriate and what implications for the meaning of mission and salvation this decision has. Generally, it would seem logical for a solution to be offered immediately after a problem has emerged. For the conceptions of mission and salvation, this means that God's offer ("sending") of a mediator between Him and humanity in the "offspring of the woman" (Gen 3:15) right after the Fall (Gen 3:6) seems to be the most logical starting point for "mission" in the Bible. It thus includes the restoration of the relationship between man and God and its implications—in other words, inner and social transformation.

At the same time, we must recognize that "mission" has different meanings in different epochs of salvation history. Of course, full-fledged mission, as understood traditionally, is possible only after the accomplishment of forgiveness of sins through Christ's death and resurrection, and after the enabling of new life through the effusion of the Spirit at Pentecost. Abraham's "mission" differs from David's task. The two differ substantially from Jesus' "mission;" and the task of the disciples is distinct from Jesus'

---

[164] Christopher J. H. Wright, "Searching for a Missional Hermeneutic," in Wright, *The Mission of God: Unlocking God's Narrative* (Downers Grove, IL: InterVarsity Press, 2006), 33–47.

"mission" even though there are many similarities.[165] Salvation equally has to be seen in the perspective of salvation history, adopting different meanings in the two testaments. The New Testament concept of salvation has to be differentiated from the Old Testament concept of *shalom* on the basis of the "eschatological interim" to be discussed in chapter 3.

## Assessment of the Biblical Analysis

The preceding review of relevant words and concepts in the Bible has shown that the same terms can denote a verbal or a non-verbal activity, or sometimes both. This is particularly the case for such activities as "preach the gospel," "evangelize," "teach," and "serve." It may be surprising to some that certain terms, which we generally classify as referring to the verbal proclamation of the gospel, sometimes also denote the whole ministry of Jesus and the apostles.

The use of certain terms in the missiological debates of the Lausanne Movement has differed somewhat from the semantic domain found in the Bible. This is the case for the Bible's use of "preach the gospel" or "evangelize" in a holistic as well as a verbal perspective, whereas the Lausanne Movement used these concepts in an exclusively verbal sense before the turn of the millennium. In the Cape Town Commitment, the non-verbal activities are rendered by the expressions "witness of life" and "transformation." This observation is also valid for the notion of sending ("mission"), which has acquired a completely new meaning in the contemporary theological and missiological discourse, covering a variety of communicative activities. For the Bible, on the other hand, sending refers to God's initiating process that underlies the communication of the gospel.

Theologians with a dichotomizing worldview tend toward narrow and well-defined semantic domains, as illustrated by the first declarations of the Lausanne Movement. They introduce distinctions and nuances in their theology and missiology, such as the distinction between evangelism and social responsibility (with priority usually given to evangelism) or between salt and light. In contrast, for theologians from the Global South who operate with a holistic worldview, a separation of different dimensions of Christian witness does not make sense. They tend toward large and fuzzy semantic domains and perceive convergences rather than divergences between the terms.

---

[165] See also Thomas Schirrmacher, *Biblical Foundations for 21st-Century World Mission. 69 Theses toward an Ongoing Global Reformation* (WEA World of Theology Series 11; Bonn: Culture and Science Publications, 2018), theses 27–31.

In the Bible, mission consists of a multiple witness: witnessing to the messianic King and his life, death, and resurrection, proclaiming the good news, making disciples of the nations, going into the whole world, baptizing in his name, teaching all that Jesus has commanded, warning of divine judgment, healing the sick, casting out demons, receiving the power of the Holy Spirit, and experiencing the presence of Christ. In other words, the components of proclamation, persuasion, dialogue, prophetic criticism, silent presence, and social action are all present in "mission."

## Conclusion

In this chapter, I have covered the missiological debate on the scope of the semantic domain of mission, the relationship between evangelism and social responsibility, and a certain conflict between theologies of the North and the South in the context of the transfer of the center of gravity of global Christianity. The traditional Western dichotomizing concept of mission has developed toward a holistic understanding of mission with the change from modernity to late modernity and the simultaneous transfer of Christianity's center of gravity toward the South and the East. The holistic conception of the majority of contextual theologies confirms this trend. I conclude that the worldview of the theologians influences their Bible interpretation and their conception of theologies of mission. In the biblical worldview, we find the dichotomizing and holistic worldviews in creative tension. These observations relativize certain theological and missiological positions and remind us to theologize within the boundaries of the biblical record.

## Further Reading

Bosch, David J., "Evangelism: Theological Currents and Cross-Currents Today," *International Bulletin of Missionary Research* 3 (1987): 98–103.

Bosch, David J., *Transforming Mission: Paradigm Shifts in Theology of Mission* (Maryknoll: Orbis, 1996), 389–447.

Hesselgrave, David J., *Paradigms in Conflict: 10 Key Questions in Christian Missions Today* (Grand Rapids: Kregel, 2005).

Schirrmacher, Thomas, *Biblical Foundations for 21st-Century World Mission: 69 Theses toward an Ongoing Global Reformation* (WEA World of Theology Series 11; Bonn: Culture and Science Publications, 2018)

# CHAPTER 3

# A Holism with Biblical Distinctions

Having reflected on evangelism and mission in the missiological, intra-evangelical debate between 1966 and 2011, the underlying worldviews, and the semantic domains of these notions in the Bible, I will conclude by analyzing the contribution of the notion of holistic mission to the missiological debate, along with its relationship to the notions of evangelism, mission, the kingdom of God, the mission of Jesus, eschatology, and the concept of multiple witness. Through this theological analysis based on the historical and biblical findings, I will propose an articulation of holism that, I believe, makes the necessary biblical distinctions.

## Positive Contribution

From a global perspective of the human being, the concept of holistic mission combines things that actually belong together. In this way, it moves beyond the dichotomizing aspects of the concept of "multiple witness" introduced by Western theologies of mission and described in the previous chapter. The same observation applies to the term "transformation" that has replaced the expression "holistic mission" in many instances. This second term helps to restore a proper biblical balance between orthodoxy and orthopraxy.[166]

## Lack of Distinctions and Nuances

Western theologians, operating generally from a dichotomizing worldview, have criticized the concept of holistic mission because it does not present the necessary distinctions. This criticism is certainly valid for Wrogemann's "identification model" that represents the WCC's position, and for Hesselgrave's "revisionist holism" that describes Bryant Myers's position. It could also apply to Hesselgrave's model of "radical liberation"

---

[166] For the transformation logic in the Bible, see Thomas Schirrmacher, *Biblical Foundations for 21st-Century World Mission. 69 Theses toward an Ongoing Global Reformation* (WEA World of Theology Series 11; Bonn: Culture and Science Publications, 2018), theses 33–34, 41, 56–64.

that includes liberation theologies. However, the criticism over lack of distinctions is certainly not valid for Wrogemann's "complementary model" and Hesselgrave's "restrained holism," both of which describe the positions of the Lausanne Movement, the Micah Network and the radical evangelicals, except perhaps for a few exceptions such as Ronald Sider's comment of 40 years ago, "The time has come for all Christians to refuse to use the sentence: 'The primary task of the Church is ... .'"[167]

The biblical worldview includes a holistic approach to the universe and life in general, with the important qualification that it conceives of the created universe as distinct from its creator. In the typology of the stratigraphic model of creation, this concept of the universe corresponds to the Hebrew worldview that places the holistic and dichotomizing worldviews in tension. As David Hesselgrave remarks, the Bible "begins with an absolute dichotomy between the Creator and his creation. It proceeds by making very different valuations of body and soul, treasures on earth and treasures in heaven, and this world and the world to come."[168] The Bible thus makes important distinctions in a generally holistic approach. The Grand Rapids Report (1982) perceives these distinctions in a rather negative way but affirms at the same time that the Bible sets them in tension:

> We tend to set over against one another in an unhealthy way soul and body, the individual and society, redemption and creation, grace and nature, heaven and earth, justification and justice, faith and works. The Bible certainly distinguishes between these, but it also relates them to each other, and it instructs us to hold each pair in a dynamic and creative tension.[169]

On the other hand, Hesselgrave sees these distinctions in a positive way and prioritizes them based on an essentially dichotomizing worldview:

> With reference to spiritual transformation and social transformation, it [the Bible] gives priority to spiritual transformation. With reference to spirit, mind, and body, it gives priority to the spirit or soul. With reference to social action and evangelism, it gives priority to evangelism. In maintaining these priorities, however, it does not admit to being reductionistic.[170]

---

[167] Ronald J. Sider, "Words and Deeds," *Journal of Theology for Southern Africa* 29 (December 1979): 47.

[168] David J. Hesselgrave, *Paradigms in Conflict: 10 Key Questions in Christian Missions Today* (Grand Rapids: Kregel, 2005), 123.

[169] Lausanne Movement, *Evangelism and Social Responsibility: An Evangelical Commitment*, Lausanne Occasional Paper 21: The Grand Rapids Report, 4A, https://www.lausanne.org/content/lop/lop-21.

[170] Hesselgrave, *Paradigms in Conflict*, 121.

Hesselgrave's remark involves the cosmological, anthropological, and soteriological dimensions of worldview. The criticism of Western theologians directed toward the term "holistic mission" due to lack of distinctions is also valid for the term "transformation." Some authors, however, distinguish between spiritual and social transformation (such as David Hesselgrave) or between inner and external transformation (Thomas Schirrmacher). Schirrmacher posits the following relationship: "From inner transformation follows external transformation, and from the transformation of individuals comes change in the broader, symbiotic community."[171] Beyond the above mentioned distinctions, we also have to introduce nuances because in missions, we find a diversity of personalities with a variety of vocations and gifts in very diverse situations and contexts.

## Evangelism and Social Responsibility

The one distinction that was most strongly emphasized in the debates within the Lausanne Movement was between evangelism and social responsibility. Other authors speak of the pair "word and deed." Stott often chose the terminology of "proclamation and presentation of the gospel," indicating the distinction between verbal and non-verbal communication of the gospel.

When discussing the terms "evangelize" (*euangelizomai*) and "preach the gospel" (*kerysso to euangelion*), we have already seen that the Bible does not particularly emphasize this distinction. Both terms can refer to the verbal communication of the gospel or to the total ministry of Jesus and the apostles, the latter of course comprising verbal communication. When the New Testament authors follow the latter logic, they are heirs to the Hebrew concept of "word" (*dabar*). The term refers to the "word in action" best shown in God's creation act: "God said ... and it was" (Gen 1:3, 6, 9, 11, 14). We find this same scheme in Jesus' ministry: his word makes things happen (e.g. Mk 5:41–42). The evangelist John reinforces this thought when he calls Jesus the Word (*logos*, Jn 1:1–4). John 1:3 spells out the implication that Jesus is the Creator-God, the "Word in action." All these examples show the unity of word and deed in the Bible.

On the other hand, already in the early church, the "ministry of the word," or the preaching ministry, together with prayer and Bible reading, is given priority by the apostles. When a problem arises about the feeding of the Greek-speaking widows, the apostles appoint deacons so that they

---

[171] Schirrmacher, *Biblical Foundations*, thesis 57.

can devote themselves "to prayer and to serving the word" (Acts 6:4).[172] With the same concern in view, Paul exhorts the Romans, "How are they to believe in one of whom they have never heard? And how are they to hear without someone to proclaim him?" (Rom 10:14). People have to hear the gospel; they cannot invent it. The apostles make thus a distinction between their "service of the word" (*diakonia tou logou*) and the (social) "service" (*diakonia*) delegated to the deacons.

In summary, we find in the Bible a tension between the unity of word and deed, on one hand, and a distinction between the ministry of the word and social ministry on the other hand. This tension is in concordance with the use of the terms "evangelize" and "preach the gospel," which can refer to the verbal communication of the gospel as well as the total ministry of Jesus and the apostles. The Micah Declaration expands the pair of "word and deed" to the triad of "being, doing, and saying." Our being and acts should confirm our words, and our words should explain our life. All the aspects of our life must be in concordance for us to function as effective witnesses to Christ. The science of communication confirms this fact by saying that only an integral communication is effective.[173]

## Eternal Destiny of Man and Holistic Mission

One aspect to which very little reflection has been devoted is the relationship between concern for people's eternal destiny and for their material and social needs. It can be very difficult to manage proclamation of the gospel and social responsibility harmoniously side by side. Social action demands a huge amount of time, energy, and financial resources and risks marginalizing the preoccupation with people's eternal destiny. In several evangelical individuals and organizations, a "drift" has been observed toward greater engagement in humanitarian responsibilities, with the result that finally no resources were left for engaging with matters of spiritual salvation.[174]

Rather than speaking about the dichotomy between evangelism and social responsibility that has animated the discussions in the Lausanne Movement, I propose another duality: on the one hand, the Bible places

---

[172] Cf. Schirrmacher, *Biblical Foundations*, theses 58 and 59.
[173] Watzlawick et al., *Pragmatics of Human Communication*, 119f.
[174] See Peirong Lin, *Countering Mission Drift in a Faith-based Organization. An Interdisciplinary Theological Interpretation Focused on the Case Study of World Vision's Identity Formation* (Bonn: Science and Culture Publications, 2019), summarized in "The Case for Practical Theological Interpretation in Faith-based Organizations," *Evangelical Review of Theology* 42, no. 4 (2018): 319–33.

great emphasis on people's eternal destiny; on the other hand, it recognizes great liberty in the choice of communicative strategies, verbal and non-verbal. We can perhaps capture this duality in the expression "Christocentric *shalom*," which combines a holistic approach with an emphasis on Christ and the salvation he offers.[175]

## Kingdom of God, Mission of God, and Holistic Mission

The introduction of the concept of holistic mission into the missiological debate has coincided with a deeper reflection on the mission of God (Latin *missio Dei*) and the kingdom of God (Greek *basileia tou theou*). During the second half of the twentieth century, these concepts have assumed an important place in missiological discourse. This has led to an enlargement of the semantic domain of mission; schematically, there has been a development from an emphasis on the acts of the disciples of Christ to God's action in the world, and from gospel preaching to actions in favor of the kingdom of God, i.e., justice and *shalom*. A biblical approach combines the two in a fruitful tension: the trinitarian God's mission and the disciples' (church's) mission, or gospel preaching and socio-political transformation.[176]

Granted, missiologists have neglected the importance of the kingdom of God previously. In the gospels, Jesus speaks of the kingdom of God more than a hundred times in relation to his person and mission, and of the Church only three times. On the other hand, Paul mentions the kingdom of God only 14 times and makes more than 40 references to the Church. Schematically speaking, the apostles founded churches as an expression of the kingdom of God and preached Jesus Christ crucified and raised, the messianic King who is building his kingdom. Thus, mission oriented toward and driven by the kingdom of God is Christ's mission. On the other hand, the disciples' mission consists of being witnesses to Christ and his reign by making disciples, preaching, baptizing and teaching (Mt 28:18–20; Mk 16:15–20; Lk 24:44-49). Whereas Jesus preaches and manifests the kingdom of God, the disciples preach Jesus and demonstrate his Lordship over all beings and things.[177]

---

[175] I am indebted to Erwan Cloarec for this expression.

[176] For a deeper discussion of the relationship between the kingdom and mission of God and the disciples' mission, see Thomas Schirrmacher, *Missio Dei: God's Missional Nature* (Bonn: Culture and Science Publications, 2017); Schirrmacher, *Biblical Foundations*, theses 1–10, 41, 56–64; Hesselgrave, *Paradigms in Conflict*, 315–56; Tennent, *Invitation to World Missions*, 53–101.

[177] I am indebted to McTair Wall for this summary statement.

## The Mission of Jesus and of the Disciples

The promoters of holistic mission see themselves as continuing Jesus' mission. According to this position, Jesus' disciples are called to "incarnate" the values of the reign of Christ in their imitation of Christ just as Jesus, the Word of God, incarnated himself in the world (Jn 1:14). Thus, Jesus' life becomes the model for the disciples' life.

However, there are aspects of discontinuity as well as continuity between the disciples' mission and that of Jesus. Obviously, Jesus was unique in his incarnation and propitiatory death on the cross. The apostle Paul sees himself as a witness to and ambassador of the unique Christ-event ("we preach Christ crucified," 1 Cor 1:23). On the other hand, he is himself an imitator of Christ and recommends this attitude to his disciples as well (1 Cor 11:1; Phil 2:5-11). According to Hesselgrave, the Bible defends the discontinuity of the different missions, and continuity only in the relationship between the Lord and his disciple:

> The Son had one mission, the Twelve another, the Seventy or Seventy-two another (Matt 10; Luke 10), and those who respond to the Great Commission of Matthew 28 and Mark 16 yet another. ... By maintaining that the church's mission is a continuation of Christ's own personal mission, [one] blurs these distinctions. ... Paul maintains continuity in the sender-sendee relationship but progression in the divine program of redemption (2 Cor 5:20).[178]

Pursuing a biblical balance, we are again called to maintain a fruitful tension between continuity and discontinuity. We imitate the aspects of Christ's mission that are not unique to Him: living in an intimate relationship with the triune God like Jesus with his Father, making disciples and communicating the gospel like Jesus. On the other hand, we are conscious of the differences between our mission and Jesus' mission: we are not the saviors of this world but Jesus' disciples; we do not build the kingdom of God ourselves, but Jesus uses us when building it.

## Eschatology and Holistic Mission

In the missiological debates, commonly very little is said about the eschatological problem of our position in the epoch between the two comings of Jesus Christ, which is called the eschatological interim. It was not Jesus' intent to heal all diseases during his life on earth. Evangelicals' energetic

---

[178] Hesselgrave, *Paradigms in Conflict*, 152.

support of the United Nations' Sustainable Development Goals could encourage us to adopt this idea. Certainly, we should be engaged in local and global efforts to alleviate suffering. But Jesus came primarily to show the character of the reign of God by his life of compassion and his signs of healing (Mt 11:4f; Lk 11:20) and to die on the cross for the sins of humanity (Mk 10:45 par.). The victory over evil and sin is already accomplished in the spiritual world, but not yet in our material world. Our struggle against sickness, misery, and poverty continues.

In this regard, biblical teaching corresponds to an inaugurated but not yet completed eschatology. The marginalization of this teaching can lead to a worldly activism that presumes that we are responsible for creating the conditions for the return of Christ (a postmillennialist position). Alternatively, it can induce an attitude of fatalism, letting world situations degenerate until God's intervention (a premillennialist position). Moreover, the lack of sound knowledge of the Bible can lead to the prosperity gospel or to dominion theology, both of which act as if the ideal state is already attained or within reach (a realized eschatology).

## Multiple Witness and Holistic Mission

To sum up its reflections on holistic mission, missiology has introduced the concept of "multiple witness." In other words, "mission" can be seen as a set of multiple witnesses: a double, triple, fourfold, or fivefold mission. We saw various applications of this concept in chapter 2.

The Anglican Communion's Five Marks of mission—proclamation, discipleship, service, socio-political transformation, and ecological involvement—are the most detailed formulation of multiple witness thus far. But even the Five Marks do not say anything about the relational dimension of mission: having coffee with our neighbor, exchanging a word of compassion with him or her in the hallway or the elevator. Even though these different efforts to go beyond the dyad of evangelism and social action indicate a development from a dichotomizing perspective toward a holistic conception of mission, they still represent the approach of theologians who make normally distinctions. This is a typical approach for analytical thinkers with a dichotomizing worldview and a rule-centered conscience. On the other hand, the proposal of a duality between a Christological and soteriological focus and a holistic approach to communicative strategies seems to embody a relational approach with some rule-centered elements. By introducing distinctions, the two approaches (a multiple witness approach and a Christological focus combined with a holistic communicative strategy) stand in opposition to conceptions of holistic mission that do not make any distinctions. This is the case with David Hesselgrave's "revisionist holism," which represents Bryant Myers's position, and with Henning Wrogemann's "identification model," which describes the WCC's position during the 1960s and 1970s. This understanding of holistic mission is thus an expression of an entirely relational conscience orientation.

## Mission as Expression of a Biblical Worldview

To round up this discussion on the notion of holistic mission, I return to the notion that our conception of mission should be an expression of a biblical worldview.

As mentioned above, there are different conceptions of holism. Promotors of holistic mission use the term in different ways. The Bible does not sustain a "revisionist holism" without any distinctions, to use Hesselgrave's terminology. Nevertheless, a "restrained holism" can be perfectly in line with a biblical worldview.

In the introduction, I proposed defining the biblical worldview by a particular configuration of four worldview models. The ideal type of the Hebrew worldview, one of the four models contained in my stratigraphic model of creation, basically sets the created universe in front of the Creator. This represents our primary concern, namely to theologize to the honor of our Creator. A second important aspect of the biblical worldview highlighted by this model consists in the biblical tension between the holistic and the dichotomizing approaches to universe and life matters. In this vein, we have seen that the Bible introduces several important dichotomies: between body and "soul/spirit," nature and grace, creation and redemption, to name just a few. Every one of these dichotomies is not absolute, as a certain unity is also found in each. In relation to creation and redemption, for example, mission will respond to the spiritual needs of man from the perspective of the "spiritual mandate" and to material and psychosocial needs through the logic of "signs of the kingdom" in the framework of the "cultural mandate." The former is distinct from the latter but operates within the latter. In a certain sense, mission can be seen as restoration of the originally intended creation order.

Concerning the five soteriological concepts, we have primarily concentrated on the notion of salvation so far. We discussed the implications of dichotomizing and holistic worldviews, and of an inaugurated rather than a realized eschatology. Even though the distinction between the spiritual and the social or physical dimensions of salvation are not clearcut, in view of the eschatological interim the distinction plays a certain role. Thus far we have not looked very much at the implications of theology proper, but they are at the center of the biblical worldview. Our triune God is the origin and the goal of mission. He is a missionary God; Jesus is the missionary *par excellence*; the Holy Spirit is the main divine communicator today.[179] This proper theological base has to be taken primarily in consideration when we reflect on the notions of evangelism and mission. In terms of anthropology, body and "soul/spirit" are distinct but combine to form a person in a "conditional unity."[180] Mission will respond to the global needs of the human being with the distinctions and priorities indicated above. In relation to hamartiology, mission will develop its "antagonistic" dimension in the light of Jesus who has come "to destroy the works of the devil" (1 Jn 3:8).[181]

In relation to conscience orientation, the Bible tells us to love God (the relational aspect) and to keep his commands (the rule-centered aspect).[182] The Bible thus proposes a balanced conscience orientation, recognizing two dimensions of mission. Its relational dimension leads us to become friends with our neighbors, drink coffee with them, take part in their areas of interest, and show compassion for their concerns. On the other hand, mission has a content dimension where we are called to communicate the biblical message of the gospel. Referring to these two dimensions, systems theory in the discipline of communication speaks of the analogous and digital modes of communication: the relationship is expressed in an analogous mode and the content in a digital mode.[183]

Concerning the biblical view of time orientation, we should aim at a balance between its efficient use in terms of punctuality and involvement with the gospel (Eph 5:16; Col 4:5) and a relaxed attitude toward time in the logic of Ecclesiastes: "There is a time for everything" (Ecc 3:1). Additionally, we search for a balance between past and future orientation, faithfulness to biblical tradition and openness for the future. The eschatological future perspective adds a missionary vision to our lives, as we are called to be active in gathering the "great multitude ... from every nation, from all tribes and peoples and languages, standing before the throne and before the Lamb" (Rev 7:9).

---

[179] Schirrmacher, *Biblical Foundations*, theses 1–10; John Stott, *The Contemporary Christian* (Downers Grove, IL: InterVarsity Press, 1992), 321–30.
[180] Millard J. Erickson, *Christian Theology* (Grand Rapids: Baker, 1983), 538–40.
[181] Peter Beyerhaus, *Er sandte sein Wort: Theologie der christlichen Mission* (Wuppertal: Brockhaus; Bad Liebenzell: VLM, 1996), 367–68.
[182] Deut 6:5f.; 7:9; 11:1, 13; 30:16; Jos 22:5; 23:6, 8; 1 Kings 9:4; Neh 1:5; Ezek 36:26f.; Dan 9:4; Jn 14:15, 21, 23f.; 15:10; 1 Jn 3:23f.
[183] Watzlawick et al., *Pragmatics of Human Communication*, 88–92.

Understanding these creative tensions and different dimensions in the biblical worldview will give us a foundation from which to address the tensions inherent in evangelism and mission.[184]

## Conclusion

In debates over the semantic domain of mission and the relationship between evangelism and social responsibility, there is an identifiable conflict between theologies of the Global North and South, which is highly relevant in the context of the present transfer of the center of gravity of global Christianity to the south and east. In addition, differing worldviews influence theologians' Bible interpretations and their conceptions of mission, although the Bible itself holds aspects of holistic and dichotomizing worldviews in tension.

One may be tempted to conclude with David Bosch that "ultimately mission remains undefinable," even in Scripture.[185] For Bosch also, the debate between evangelical and ecumenical voices shows the influence of differing worldviews. Bosch assesses the competing views as partial and complementary.[186] The debates over evangelism, social responsibility, and mission in the Lausanne Movement indicate an analogous explanation for the differing positions of theologians from the Global North and South. Generally speaking, the former group leans towards a dichotomizing and the latter towards a more holistic worldview. My biblical analysis seems to confirm Bosch's perspective in this regard.

These debates show the importance of faithful anchoring in the biblical text and deep understanding of the biblical worldview. I propose that we can gain a suitably broad grasp of the biblical worldview by integrating four models: the Hebrew worldview within the stratigraphic model of creation, a biblical configuration of the five soteriological concepts (God, man evil, sin and salvation), and a balanced conscience and time orientation.

Overall, the biblical record assures us that the different dimensions of Christian witness are all important. Words explain being and acts, and the latter confirm the words. At the same time, the Bible's preoccupation with the eternal destiny of man, and the liberty of God and his envoys in their choice of communicative strategies, should orient our understanding of evangelism and mission.

---

[184] For a more detailed discussion of a biblical worldview, cf. Wiher, "Worldview and Identity across Conversion," 307–16.

[185] Bosch, *Transforming Mission*, 9.

[186] David Bosch, *Witness to the World: The Christian Mission in Theological Perspective* (Atlanta: John Knox Press; London: Marshall, Morgan & Scott, 1980), 202–20.

# Bibliography

## Evangelical Conference Documents and Declarations

All the documents of the Lausanne Movement (Declarations and Lausanne Occasional Papers, LOPs) can be found on their website: https://www.lausanne.org/category/content.

### Wheaton (1966)

"Wheaton Declaration," *International Review of Mission* 55, no. 220 (1966): 458–76.

*Study Papers: Congress on the Church's Worldwide Mission, April 9–16, 1966, Wheaton, Illinois* (Wheaton: Scripture Press Foundation, 1966).

"Records of the World Congress on Evangelism: Collection 14," www.wheaton.edu/bgc/archives/guides/014.htm#3.

### Berlin (1966)

Henry, Carl F. H., and W. Stanley Mooneyham, eds., *One Race, One Gospel, One Task: World Congress on Evangelism, Berlin 1966*, vol. 1 (Minneapolis: World Wide Publications, 1967).

### Frankfurt (1970)

"Frankfurt Declaration on the Fundamental Crisis of Mission," *Christianity Today* June 19 (1970): 3–6.

Beyerhaus, Peter. *Krise und Neuaufbruch der Weltmission* (Bad Liebenzell: VLM, 1985).

### Lausanne (1974)

Douglas, James D., *Let the Earth Hear His Voice: Official Reference Volume, Papers and Responses*, International Congress on World Evangelization Lausanne (Minneapolis: World Wide Publications, 1975).

Stott, John, *The Lausanne Covenant: An Exposition and Commentary* (Minneapolis: World Wide Publications, 1975).

"Lausanne Declaration," https://www.lausanne.org/content/covenant/lausanne-covenant.

## Pattaya (1980)

Robinson, J. F., ed., *How Shall They Hear? Consultation on World Evangelization. Official Reference Volume. Thailand Reports*, Wheaton, Lausanne Committee for World Evangelization, 1980.

## Hoddesdon (1980)

"An Evangelical Commitment to Simple Lifestyle," *Occasional Bulletin of Missionary Research* 4, no. 4 (1980): 177–79.

Lausanne Occasional Paper 20.

## Grand Rapids (1982)

"The Grand Rapids Report on Evangelism and Social Responsibility: An Evangelical Commitment," in John Stott, *Making Christ Known: Historic Mission Documents from the Lausanne Movement 1974–1989* (Grand Rapids: Eerdmans, 1996), 185–219.

Lausanne Occasional Paper 21.

## Wheaton (1983)

Samuel, Vinay, and Chris Sugden, eds., *The Church in Response to Human Need* (Grand Rapids: Eerdmans, 1987).

## Manila (1989)

Douglas, James D., ed., *Proclaim Christ Until He Comes. Calling the Whole Church to Take the Whole Gospel to the Whole World*, Lausanne II International Congress on World Evangelization in Manila 1989 (Minneapolis: World Wide Publications, 1990).

"The Manila Manifesto," https://www.lausanne.org/content/manifesto/the-manila-manifesto.

## Oxford (2001)

"Micah Declaration on Integral Mission," https://www.micahnetwork.org/?s=micah%20+declaration+on+integral+mission.

## Pattaya (2004)

Lausanne Occasional Paper 33.

## Cape Town (2010)

"The Cape Town Commitment: A Confession of Faith and a Call to Action," https://www.lausanne.org/content/ctcommitment#capetown.

## Bangkok (2011)

"Christian Witness in a Multi-Religious World," https://www.worldevangelicals.org/pdf/1106Christian_Witness_in_a_Multi-Religious_World.pdf.

## Works Cited

Bassham, Rodger C., *Mission Theology: 1948-1975, Years of Worldwide Creative Tension: Ecumenical, Evangelical, and Roman Catholic* (Pasadena, CA: William Carey Library, 1979).

Bastian, Jean-Pierre, Françoise Champion, and Kathy Rousselet, eds., *La globalisation du religieux* (Paris: l'Harmattan, 2001).

Bavinck, Johan H., *An Introduction to the Science of Missions* (Philadelphia: Presbyterian and Reformed, 1960).

Becker, Ulrich, "Gospel, Evangelize, Evangelist," in *New International Dictionary of the New Testament*, vol. 2, ed. Colin Brown, rev. ed. (Carlisle, UK: Paternoster; Grand Rapids, MI: Zondervan, 1986), 107-115.

Berneburg, Erhard, *Das Verhältnis von Verkündigung und sozialer Aktion in der evangelikalen Missionstheorie* (Wuppertal: Brockhaus, 1997).

Beyerhaus, Peter, "Mission and Humanization," *International Review of Mission* 60, no. 237 (1971): 11-24.

Beyerhaus, Peter, *Krise und Neuaufbruch der Weltmission* (Bad Liebenzell, VLM, 1987).

Beyerhaus, Peter, *Er sandte sein Wort: Theologie der christlichen Mission* (Wuppertal: Brockhaus; Bad Liebenzell: VLM, 1996).

Blocher, Henri, "John Stott, Mr Evangelical," *Perspectives missionnaires* 62 (2011): 37-41.

Bonny, Yves, *Sociologie du temps présent. Modernité avancée ou postmodernité?* (Paris: Armand Colin, 2004).

Bosch, David J., *Witness to the World: The Christian Mission in Theological Perspective* (Atlanta: John Knox Press, London: Marshall, Morgan & Scott, 1980).

Bosch, David, "An Emerging Paradigm for Mission," *Missiology* 11, no. 4 (1983): 485-510.

Bosch, David J., "Evangelism: Theological Currents and Cross-Currents Today," *International Bulletin of Missionary Research* 3 (1987): 98-103.

Bosch, David J., *Transforming Mission: Paradigm Shifts in Theology of Mission* (Maryknoll: Orbis, 1991).

Braaten, Carl, *The Apostolic Imperative: Nature and Aim of the Church's Mission and Ministry* (Minneapolis: Augsburg, 1985).

Bujo, Bénézet, *African Theology in its Social Context* (Nairobi: St. Paul-Africa, 1992).

Calvin, John, *Institution of the Christian Religion* (London: Harrison, 1561).

Carpenter, Joel, and Wilbert Shenk, *Earthen Vessels: American Evangelicals and Foreign Missions 1880-1980* (Grand Rapids: Eerdmans, 1990).

Carroll, Lewis, *Through the Looking-Glass* (Raleigh, NC: Hayes Barton Press, 1872).

Castro, Emilio, "Evangelism and Social Justice," *Ecumenical Review* 20, no. 2 (1968): 146–150.

Černý, Pavel, "John Stott (1921–2011), Radical Disciple of Christ: On the Centenary of His Birth and the Tenth Anniversary of His Death," *European Journal of Theology* 30, no. 1 (2021), 7–17.

Chester, Timothy, *Awakening to a World of Need: The Recovery of Evangelical Social Concern* (Leicester: IVP, 1993).

Chilcote, Paul W., and Laceye C. Warner, eds., *The Study of Evangelism: Exploring a Missional Practice of the Church* (Grand Rapids: Eerdmans, 2008).

Coupland, Douglas, *Generation X: Tales for Accelerated Culture* (London: Abacus, 1996).

Donovan, Kath, and Ruth Myors, "A Generational Perspective into the Future," in *Too Valuable to Lose: Exploring the Causes and Cures of Missionary Attrition*, ed. William D. Taylor (Pasadena, CA: William Carey Library, 1997) 41–73.

Douglas, James D., *Let the Earth Hear His Voice: Official Reference Volume, Papers and Responses*, International Congress on World Evangelization Lausanne (Minneapolis: World Wide Publications, 1975).

Engel, James F., and William A. Dyrness, *Changing the Mind of Missions: Where Have We Gone Wrong?* (Downers Grove: IVP, 2000)

Engelsviken, Tormod, "Mission, Evangelism and Evangelization. From the Perspective of the Lausanne Movement," *International Review of Mission* 96 (2007): 204–9.

Ericksen, Paul, "Interview with René Padilla, Billy Graham Center," https://www2.wheaton.edu/bgc/archives/transcripts/cn361t03.pdf.

Erickson, Millard J., *Christian Theology* (Grand Rapids: Baker, 1983).

Escobar, Samuel, "A Movement Divided. Three Approaches to World Evangelization Stand in Tension with One Another," *Transformation* 8, no. 4 (1991): 7–13.

Escobar, Samuel, "Latin American Theology," in *Dictionary of Mission Theology: Evangelical Foundations*, ed. John Corrie, Samuel Escobar, and Wilbert Shenk (Downers Grove, IL: IVP, 2007), 203–7.

Escobar, Samuel and John Driver, *Christian Mission and Social Justice* (Scottdale, PA: Herald, 1978).

Ferry, Luc, *Homo œstheticus. L'invention du goût à l'âge démocratique* (Paris: Grasset, 1990).

Geertz, Clifford, *The Interpretation of Cultures* (New York: Basic Books, 1973).

Gener, Timoteo D., and Stephen D. Pardue (eds.), *Asian Christian Theology: Evangelical Perspectives* (Carlisle, UK: Langham Global Library, 2019).

Glasser, Arthur F., "The Evolution of Evangelical Mission Theology since World War II," *International Bulletin of Missionary Research* 6 (1985): 9–13.

Graham, Billy, "Why Berlin 1966?" in *One Race, One Gospel, One Task: World Congress on Evangelism, Berlin 1966*, vol. 1, ed. Carl F. H. Henry and W. Stanley Mooneyham (Minneapolis: World Wide Publications, 1967), 25–29.

Graham, Billy, "Why Lausanne?" in *Let the Earth Hear His Voice: Official Reference Volume, Papers and Responses*, International Congress on World Evangelization Lausanne, ed. James D. Douglas (Minneapolis: World Wide Publications, 1975), 22–36.

Hedlund, Roger, *Roots of the Great Debate in Mission* (Bangalore, India: Theological Book Trust, 1997).

Henry, Carl F. H., *The Uneasy Conscience of Modern Fundamentalism* (Grand Rapids: Eerdmans, 1947).

Henry, Carl F. H., *Evangelical Responsibility in Contemporary Theology* (Grand Rapids: Eerdmans, 1957).

Henry, Carl F. H., and W. Stanley Mooneyham, eds., *One Race, One Gospel, One Task: World Congress on Evangelism, Berlin 1966*, vol. 1 (Minneapolis: World Wide Publications, 1967).

Hesselgrave, David J., *Paradigms in Conflict: 10 Key Questions in Christian Missions Today* (Grand Rapids: Kregel, 2005).

Hiebert, Paul G., "The Flaw of the Excluded Middle," *Missiology: An International Review* 10, no. 1 (1982): 35–47.

Hiebert, Paul G., *Anthropological Insights for Missionaries* (Grand Rapids: Baker, 1985).

Hiebert, Paul G., *Transforming Worldviews: An Anthropological Understanding of How People Change* (Grand Rapids: Baker, 2008).

Hiebert, Paul G., Daniel R. Shaw, Tite Tiénou, *Understanding Folk Religion: A Christian Response to Popular Beliefs and Practices* (Grand Rapids: Baker, 1999).

Hoekendijk, Johannes, *The Church Inside Out* (London: SCM, 1967).

Hunt, Robert A., "The History of the Lausanne Movement," *International Bulletin of Missionary Research* 35, no. 2 (2011): 81–86.

Huntington, Samuel P., *The Clash of Civilizations and the Remaking of World Order* (New York: Free Press, 1997).

Johnston, Arthur P., *The Battle for World Evangelization* (Wheaton: Tyndale, 1978).

Käser, Lothar, *Foreign Cultures: An Introduction to Ethnology* (Nuremberg: VTR, 2014).

Kant, Immanuel, *Critique of the Power of Judgment*, ed. and trans. Paul Guyer (1790; Cambridge: Cambridge University Press, 2008).

Kirkpatrick, David C., "C. René Padilla and the Origins of Integral Mission in Post-War Latin America," *Journal of Ecclesiastical History* 67, no. 2 (2016): 351–71.

Kirkpatrick, David C., "The Widening of Christian Mission: C. René Padilla and the Intellectual Origins of Integral Mission," in *The End of Theology: Shaping Theology for the Sake of Mission*, ed. Jason S. Sexton and Paul Weston (Minneapolis: Fortress, 2016), 193–210.

Kirkpatrick, David C., *A Gospel for the Poor: Global Social Christianity and the Latin American Evangelical Left* (Philadelphia: University of Pennsylvania Press, 2019).

Latourette, Kenneth S., "Ecumenical Bearings of the Missionary Movement and the International Missionary Council," in *A History of the Ecumenical Movement, vol. 1: 1517-1948*, ed. Ruth Rouse and Stephen C. Neill (Geneva: World Council of Churches, 1993), 353–402.

Lin, Peirong, "The Case for Practical Theological Interpretation in Faith-based Organizations," *Evangelical Review of Theology* 42, no. 4 (2018): 319–33.

Lin, Peirong, *Countering Mission Drift in a Faith-based Organization. An Interdisciplinary Theological Interpretation Focused on the Case Study of World Vision's Identity Formation* (Bonn: Culture and Science Publications, 2019).

Lindsell, Harold, "A Rejoinder," *International Review of Mission* 54 (October 1965): 437–40.

Lingenfelter, Sherwood G., and Marvin K. Mayers, *Ministering Cross-Culturally. An Incarnational Model for Personal Relationships* (Grand Rapids: Baker Academic, 1986, 2003).

Lipovetsky, Gilles, *Hypermodern Times* (Cambridge: Polity Press, 2005).

Livingston, J. Kevin, "A Missiology of the Road: The Theology of Mission and Evangelism of David J. Bosch," Ph.D. thesis, University of Aberdeen, 1989.

Marsden, George M., *Fundamentalism and American Culture: The Shaping of Twentieth Century Evangelicalism, 1870-1925* (New York and Oxford: Oxford University Press, 1980).

Matthey, Jacques, "Édimbourg 1910 et son approche de la relation entre mission et unité," *Histoire et missions chrétiennes* no. 13 (2010): 71–92.

McGavran, Donald, "Missiology Faces the Lion," *Missiology* 17, no. 3 (1989): 335–56.

Mission and Evangelism Commission of the World Council of Churches, *Together towards Life: Mission and Evangelism in Changing Landscapes: A New WCC Affirmation on Mission and Evangelism* (Geneva: WCC, 2013).

Moberg, David O., *The Great Reversal: Evangelism versus Social Concern* (Philadelphia and New York: Lippincott, 1972).

Mombo, Esther, "From Fourfold Mission to Holistic Mission: Towards Edinburgh 2010," in *Holistic Mission. God's Plan for God's People*, ed. Brian Woolnough and Wonsuk Ma (Oxford: Regnum, 2010), 37–46.

Myers, Bryant, *Walking with the Poor: Principles and Practices of Transformational Development* (Monrovia, CA: World Vision, 1999).

Myers, Bryant, "Holistic Mission: New Frontiers," in *Holistic Mission. God's Plan for God's People*, ed. Brian Woolnough and Wonsuk Ma (Oxford: Regnum, 2010), 119–27.

Naugle, David K., *Worldview: The History of a Concept* (Grand Rapids: Eerdmans, 2001).

Nederveen Pieterse, Jan, *Globalization and Culture: Global Mélange*, 2nd ed. (New York: Rowman & Littlefield, 2009).

Neill, Stephen C., *Creative Tension* (London: Edinburgh House, 1959).

Newbigin, Lesslie, *One Body, One Gospel, One World: The Christian Mission Today* (London and New York: International Missionary Council, 1958).

Ott, Craig, "Globalization and Contextualization: Reframing the Task of Contextualization in the Twenty-First Century," *Missiology* 43, no. 1 (2015): 43–58.

Padilla, C. René, "Evangelism and Social Responsibility: From Wheaton '66 to Wheaton '83," *Transformation* 2, no. 3 (1985): 27–34.

Padilla, C. Rene, "Holistic Mission," in *Dictionary of Mission Theology: Evangelical Foundations*, ed. John Corrie, Samuel Escobar, Wilbert Shenk (Downers Grove: IVP, 2007), 157–62.

Padilla, C. René, "The Future of the Lausanne Movement," *International Bulletin of Missionary Research* 35, no. 2 (2011): 86–88.

Padilla, C. René, "Global Partnership and Integral Mission," in *Mission in Context: Explorations Inspired by J. Andrew Kirk*, ed. John Corrie and Cathy Ross (Farnham: Ashgate, 2012), 47–60.

Padilla, René, and Chris Sugden, eds., *Texts on Evangelical Social Ethics 1974-1983* (Nottingham, UK: Grove, 1985).

Pierson, Paul E., "Lessons from the Twentieth Century: Conciliar Missions," in *Between Past and Future: Evangelical Mission Entering the Twenty-first Century*, ed. Jonathan Bonk (Pasadena, CA: William Carey Library, 2003), 67–84.

Polanyi, Michael, *Personal Knowledge: Towards a Post-Critical Philosophy* (Chicago: University of Chicago Press, 1958).

Polanyi, Michael, *The Tacit Dimension* (Garden City, NY: Doubleday, 1966).

Rempp, Jean-Paul, "Le Mouvement de Lausanne après le Cap: Évolution et perspectives," *Théologie évangélique* 11, no. 3 (2012): 125–202.

Ritzer, George, *The McDonaldization of Society* (Thousand Oaks, CA: Pine Forge, 1993).

Robertson, Roland, "Glocalization: Time-Space and Homogeneity-Heterogeneity," in *Global Modernities*, ed. M. Featherstone, S. Lash, and R. Robertson (Thousand Oaks, CA: Sage, 1995), 25–44.

Samuel, Vinay, and Chris Sugden, eds., *The Church in Response to Human Need* (Grand Rapids: Eerdmans, 1987).

Scherer, James A., *Gospel, Church and Kingdom: Comparative Studies in World Mission Theology* (Minneapolis: Augsburg, 1987).

Scherer, James A., and Stephen B. Bevans, eds., *New Directions in Mission and Evangelization*, vol. 2: *Theological Foundations* (Maryknoll, NY: Orbis, 1994).

Schirrmacher, Thomas, *Missio Dei: God's Missional Nature* (WEA World of Theology Series 10; Bonn: Culture and Science Publications, 2017). Original German version 1993, original English version 1994.

Schirrmacher, Thomas, *Biblical Foundations for 21st-Century World Mission. 69 Theses toward an Ongoing Global Reformation* (WEA World of Theology Series 11; Bonn: Culture and Science Publications, 2018).

Schreiter, Robert J., "From the Lausanne Covenant to the Cape Town Commitment: A Theological Assessment," *International Bulletin of Missionary Research* 35, no. 2 (2011): 88–92.

Shaw, R. Daniel, "Beyond Syncretism: A Dynamic Approach to Hybridity," *International Bulletin of Mission Research* 42, no. 1 (2018): 6–19.

Shenk, Wilbert R., "2004 Forum for World Evangelization: A Report," *International Bulletin of Missionary Research* 29, no. 2 (2005): 31.

Sider, Ronald J., "Words and Deeds," *Journal of Theology for Southern Africa* 29 (December 1979): 47–56.

Sider, Ronald J., *Good News and Good Works: A Theology for the Whole Gospel* (Grand Rapids: Baker, 1999).

Sider, Ronald J., "Evangelism, Salvation, and Social Justice," in *The Study of Evangelism: Exploring a Missional Practice of the Church*, ed. Paul W. Chilcote and Laceye C. Warner (Grand Rapids: Eerdmans, 2008), 185–204.

Smith, Timothy L., "Recent Historical Perspectives of the Evangelical Tradition," in *Christian Relief and Development: Developing Workers for Effective Ministry*, ed. Edgar J. Elliston (Dallas: Word, 1989), 9–30.

Steuernagel, Valdir R., "Social Concern and Evangelization: The Journey of the Lausanne Movement," *Occasional Bulletin from the Missionary Research Library* 15, no. 2 (1975).

Steuernagel, Valdir R., "The Theology of Mission in Its Relation to Social Responsibility within the Lausanne Movement," Ph.D. thesis, Lutheran School of Theology, Chicago, 1988.

Stott, John, "The Great Commission," in *One Race, One Gospel, One Task: World Congress on Evangelism, Berlin 1966*, vol. 1, ed. Carl F. H. Henry and W. Stanley Mooneyham (Minneapolis: World Wide Publications, 1967), 35–39.

Stott, John, "Biblical Basis of Evangelism," in *Let the Earth Hear His Voice: Official Reference Volume, Papers and Responses*, International Congress on World Evangelization Lausanne, ed. James D. Douglas (Minneapolis: World Wide Publications, 1975), 65–78.

Stott, John, *Christian Mission in the Modern World* (Downers Grove: IVP, 2013; 1st ed. London: Falcon, 1975).

Stott, John, *The Lausanne Covenant: An Exposition and Commentary* (Minneapolis: World Wide Publications, 1975).

Stott, John, "Significance of Lausanne," *International Review of Mission* 64, no. 255 (1975): 288–94.

Stott, John, "Holistic Mission," in Stott, *The Contemporary Christian: Applying God's Word to Today's World* (Downers Grove: IVP, 1992), 343-349.

Stott, John, "Twenty Years after Lausanne: Some Personal Reflections," *International Bulletin of Missionary Research* 19, no. 1 (1995): 50–55.

Stott, John, *Making Christ Known: Historic Mission Documents from the Lausanne Movement 1974-1989* (Grand Rapids: Eerdmans, 1996).

Strauss, William, and Neil Howe, *Generations: The History of America's Future, 1584 to 2069* (New York: Quill, 1992).

Sugden, Christopher, "Theological Developments since Lausanne I," *Transformation* 7, no. 1 (1990): 9–12.

Sugden, Christopher, "Transformational Development: Current State of Understanding and Practice," *Transformation* 20, no. 2 (2003): 71–77.

Tennent, Timothy C., *Invitation to World Missions: A Trinitarian Missiology for the Twenty-first Century* (Grand Rapids: Zondervan, 2010).

Tizon, Al, *Transformation after Lausanne* (Carlisle, UK and Waynesboro, GA: Regnum, 2008).

Tizon, Al, "Precursors and Tensions in Holistic Mission: An Historical Overview," in *Holistic Mission: God's Plan for God's People*, eds. Brian Woolnough and Wonsuk Ma (Regnum Edinburgh 2010 Series; Oxford: Regnum, 2010), 61–75.

Utuk, Efiong S., "From Wheaton to Lausanne," in *New Directions in Mission and Evangelization*, vol. 2: *Theological Foundations*, ed. James A. Scherer and Stephen B. Bevans (Maryknoll, NY: Orbis, 1994), 95–114.

Van de Poll, Evert, "Témoignage multiple. La mission intégrale en quatre mandats," in *Mission intégrale: Vivre, annoncer et manifester l'Évangile pour que le monde croie* (Charols: Excelsis, 2017), 59–84.

Van Engen, Charles, *Mission on the Way. Issues in Mission Theology* (Grand Rapids: Baker, 1996).

Visser 't Hooft, Willem A., "Jesus Is Lord: The Kingship of Christ in the Bible," *Theology Today* vol. 4, no. 2 (1947): 177–89.

Walls, Andrew F., "Christian Mission in a Five-Hundred-Year Context," in *Mission in the 21st Century: Exploring the Five Marks of Global Mission*, ed. Andrew F. Walls and Cathy Ross (London: Darton, Longman & Todd, 2008), 193–204.

Walls, Andrew F., "From Christendom to World Christianity: Missions and the Demographic Transformation of the Church," in *The Cross-Cultural Process in Christian History* (Maryknoll: Orbis, 2002), 49–71.

Walls, Andrew F., and Cathy Ross, eds., *Mission in the 21st Century: Exploring the Five Marks of Global Mission* (London: Darton, Longman & Todd, 2008).

Watzlawick, Paul, Janet H. Helminck-Beavin, and Don D. Jackson, *Pragmatics of Human Communication: A Study of Interactional Patterns, Pathologies, and Paradoxes* (New York: W. W. Norton & Co., 1967).

White, James E., *Meet Generation Z. Understanding and Reaching the New Post-Christian World* (Grand Rapids, MI: Baker, 2017).

Wiher, Hannes, *Shame and Guilt. A Key to Cross-Cultural Ministry* (Bonn: Culture and Science Publications, 2003).

Wiher, Hannes, "Worldview and Identity across Conversion," *Evangelical Review of Theology* 38, no. 4 (2014): 307–23.

# Bibliography

Winter, Ralph, "The Highest Priority: Cross-Cultural Evangelism," in *Let the Earth Hear His Voice: Official Reference Volume, Papers and Responses*, International Congress on World Evangelization Lausanne, ed. James D. Douglas (Minneapolis: World Wide Publications, 1975), 213-225.

Wittgenstein, Ludwig, *Philosophical Investigations*, 2nd ed., trans. G. Anscombe (Oxford: Blackwell, 1972).

Woolnough, Brian, and Wonsuk Ma, eds., *Holistic Mission: God's Plan for God's People* (Regnum Edinburgh 2010 Series; Oxford: Regnum, 2010), https://digitalshowcase.oru.edu/cgi/viewcontent.cgi?article=1010&context=re2010series.

Wright, Christopher J. H., *The Five Marks of Mission* (London: Impress, 2015).

Wright, Christopher J. H., "Searching for a Missional Hermeneutic," in *The Mission of God: Unlocking God's Narrative* (Downers Grove: IVP, 2006), 33–47.

Wrogemann, Henning, *Intercultural Theology*, vol. 2: *Theologies of Mission* (Downers Grove: IVP Academic, 2018).

## World Evangelical Alliance

World Evangelical Alliance is a global ministry working with local churches around the world to join in common concern to live and proclaim the Good News of Jesus in their communities. WEA is a network of churches in 129 nations that have each formed an evangelical alliance and over 100 international organizations joining together to give a worldwide identity, voice and platform to more than 600 million evangelical Christians. Seeking holiness, justice and renewal at every level of society – individual, family, community and culture, God is glorified and the nations of the earth are forever transformed.

Christians from ten countries met in London in 1846 for the purpose of launching, in their own words, "a new thing in church history, a definite organization for the expression of unity amongst Christian individuals belonging to different churches." This was the beginning of a vision that was fulfilled in 1951 when believers from 21 countries officially formed the World Evangelical Fellowship. Today, 150 years after the London gathering, WEA is a dynamic global structure for unity and action that embraces 600 million evangelicals in 129 countries. It is a unity based on the historic Christian faith expressed in the evangelical tradition. And it looks to the future with vision to accomplish God's purposes in discipling the nations for Jesus Christ.

Commissions:

- Theology
- Missions
- Religious Liberty
- Women's Concerns
- Youth
- Information Technology

Initiatives and Activities

- Ambassador for Human Rights
- Ambassador for Refugees
- Creation Care Task Force
- Global Generosity Network
- International Institute for Religious Freedom
- International Institute for Islamic Studies
- Leadership Institute
- Micah Challenge
- Global Human Trafficking Task Force
- Peace and Reconciliation Initiative
- UN-Team

Church Street Station
P.O. Box 3402
New York, NY 10008-3402
Phone +[1] 212 233 3046
Fax +[1] 646-957-9218
www.worldea.org

## Giving Hands

GIVING HANDS GERMANY (GH) was established in 1995 and is officially recognized as a nonprofit foreign aid organization. It is an international operating charity that – up to now – has been supporting projects in about 40 countries on four continents. In particular we care for orphans and street children. Our major focus is on Africa and Central America. GIVING HANDS always mainly provides assistance for self-help and furthers human rights thinking.

The charity itself is not bound to any church, but on the spot we are co-operating with churches of all denominations. Naturally we also cooperate with other charities as well as governmental organizations to provide assistance as effective as possible under the given circumstances.

The work of GIVING HANDS GERMANY is controlled by a supervisory board. Members of this board are Manfred Feldmann, Colonel V. Doner and Kathleen McCall. Dr. Christine Schirrmacher is registered as legal manager of GIVING HANDS at the local district court. The local office and work of the charity are coordinated by Rev. Horst J. Kreie as executive manager. Dr. theol. Thomas Schirrmacher serves as a special consultant for all projects.

Thanks to our international contacts companies and organizations from many countries time and again provide containers with gifts in kind which we send to the different destinations where these goods help to satisfy elementary needs. This statutory purpose is put into practice by granting nutrition, clothing, education, construction and maintenance of training centers at home and abroad, construction of wells and operation of water treatment systems, guidance for self-help and transportation of goods and gifts to areas and countries where needy people live.

GIVING HANDS has a publishing arm under the leadership of Titus Vogt, that publishes human rights and other books in English, Spanish, Swahili and other languages.

These aims are aspired to the glory of the Lord according to the basic Christian principles put down in the Holy Bible.

Baumschulallee 3a • D-53115 Bonn • Germany
Phone: +49 / 228 / 695531 • Fax +49 / 228 / 695532
www.gebende-haende.de • info@gebende-haende.de

# Martin Bucer Seminary

**Faithful to biblical truth**
**Cooperating with the Evangelical Alliance**
**Reformed**

## Solid training for the Kingdom of God
- Alternative theological education
- Study while serving a church or working another job
- Enables students to remain in their own churches
- Encourages independent thinking
- Learning from the growth of the universal church.

## Academic
- For the Bachelor's degree: 180 Bologna-Credits
- For the Master's degree: 120 additional Credits
- Both old and new teaching methods: All day seminars, independent study, term papers, etc.

## Our Orientation:
- Complete trust in the reliability of the Bible
- Building on reformation theology
- Based on the confession of the German Evangelical Alliance
- Open for innovations in the Kingdom of God

## Our Emphasis:
- The Bible
- Ethics and Basic Theology
- Missions
- The Church

## Our Style:
- Innovative
- Relevant to society
- International
- Research oriented
- Interdisciplinary

## Structure
- 15 study centers in 7 countries with local partners
- 5 research institutes
- President: Prof. Dr. Thomas Schirrmacher
  Vice President: Prof. Dr. Thomas K. Johnson
- Deans: Thomas Kinker, Th.D.;
  Titus Vogt, lic. theol., Carsten Friedrich, M.Th.

## Missions through research
- Institute for Religious Freedom
- Institute for Islamic Studies
- Institute for Life and Family Studies
- Institute for Crisis, Dying, and Grief Counseling
- Institute for Pastoral Care

www.bucer.eu • info@bucer.eu

Berlin I Bielefeld I Bonn I Chemnitz I Hamburg I Munich I Pforzheim
Innsbruck I Istanbul I Izmir I Linz I Prague I São Paulo I Tirana I Zurich

www.ingramcontent.com/pod-product-compliance
Lightning Source LLC
Chambersburg PA
CBHW070306100426
42743CB00011B/2376